Joseph Maximilian Hark

The Unity of the Truth in Christianity and Evolution

Joseph Maximilian Hark

The Unity of the Truth in Christianity and Evolution

ISBN/EAN: 9783337165291

Printed in Europe, USA, Canada, Australia, Japan

Cover: Foto ©Lupo / pixelio.de

More available books at **www.hansebooks.com**

THE

UNITY OF THE TRUTH

IN

CHRISTIANITY AND EVOLUTION.

BY

J. MAX HARK, D.D.

NEW YORK:

JOHN. B. ALDEN, PUBLISHER.

1888.

LYMAN ABBOTT, D.D.

MY DEAR BROTHER:

To you I beg in gratitude to inscribe this little volume. If there is any worth in it, it is owing to the lessons in Christian thinking—even rarer in the world than Christian conduct—derived from the spirit of your writings. If it has no worth, it but proves me an inapt scholar in learning and practicing those lessons. In either case, you, I know, will be the one first to approve or to forgive, and the last one to doubt the motives of him who shall ever remain

Gratefully Yours,

J. MAX HARK.

Lancaster, Pa., March, 1888.

PREFACE.

IN the preface to his latest volume of published sermons, "The Appeal to Life," which has been a help and an inspiration to thousands, Dr. T. T. Munger refers to the "vast number who are asking if they can think under the principle of evolution and also as Christian believers," and expresses his conviction that "the necessity of showing the possibility of this . . . . is the most imperative work now pressing upon religious teachers who are able to discern the signs of the times, and who would serve their day and generation." My experience for a long time has been pressing this same conviction upon me with daily increasing urgency and force. People are coming to me, more and more frequently from year to year, with that same question; people of all classes, —many professional men, more business men, most of all mechanics and working men,—and especially young people. Good, devout Christians come in deep distress, after listening at some lyceum or in some private gathering to the disciple of Ingersoll, who in the popular

name of Evolution, distorting a few facts of
science, has been rudely shaking their faith in
God who is a Spirit, in Christ Jesus their
Saviour, and in the very existence of their own
souls;—they come anxiously inquiring, "Are
these things so?" It will not do merely to say
"No!" They have heard professed facts, even
though in wrong relations; and they must be
given deeper, broader facts, in right relations,
to have their peace of mind restored. Others
again come whose conviction of the truth of
the principle of Evolution is so deep that, when
they read in some theological journal such mis-
interpretations of the vital truths of Christianity as make religion totally incompatible with
those of their philosophy, they feel that they
must give up one or the other. They simply
cannot renounce their convictions. They dare
not and would not deny their faith. What
shall they do? Can I not help them? I feel
that they must be helped or they inevitably
will sink into that state of spiritual apathy and
listlessness in which, while holding to the forms
of Christianity, they have lost all living interest
in its eternal realities;—they will join the great
crowd of unthinking ecclesiastical formalists,
who hold to their creeds with their lips, but

upon whose life and character Christianity has
no true hold, and exerts no potent, saving influence.

Again and again have I been asked by such
persons, honest, earnest, sincere men, and
women too, whether there were not some work
that I could recommend which would meet
their wants: short enough for busy people to
read, yet comprehensive enough to explain the
essential principles of Christianity and of Evolution, and to show their true relations; plain
and untechnical enough for unscientific and
untheological persons to understand; and, above
all, fair enough, both to Christianity and to
Evolution, for honest, thinking men to appre-
ciate. I knew of no single work that fulfilled
all these conditions. Yet I believe that similar
inquiries are being made and the same want
felt all over the country. So I have tried to
make just such a work, embodying in it the results of fifteen years of earnest, often anxious,
study on the subject,—results arrived at gradually, after going through all the doubts and
struggles in my own experience in which thousands everywhere are still engaged. To me
these results have brought the profound satisfaction and peace of clear conviction. If they

shall do the same to others, bringing calm
where before was unrest, light where before
was darkness; if they shall in any degree help
them to a knowledge of that Truth which shall
make them free, then my labor shall not have
been unrewarded, nor my prayers without their
answer.

CONTENTS.

I.

INTRODUCTORY.

" No terms make I with Bigot, none with blind
Credulity, who leads the blind astray,
But rational Religion is my friend,
And I am hers, and her supporter bold.

. . . . .

I but prepare the world for larger faith;
The doubt I plant stakes up the vine belief,
And Christ sits firmer on his kingdom's throne
Because of Science."
(W. H. VENABLE—A Vision of Science.)

"In presence of the theological thaw going on so fast on
all sides, there is on the part of many a fear, and on the
part of some a hope, that nothing will remain. But the
hopes and the fears are alike groundless. . . . .
Like the transformations that have succeeded one another
hitherto, the transformation now in progress is but an advance from a lower form, no longer fit, to a higher and
fitter form."
(HERBERT SPENCER—The Study of Sociology.)

"Christianity being stationary and authoritative, thought
progressive and independent, the causes which stimulate
the restlessness of the latter interrupt the harmony which
ordinarily exists between belief and knowledge, and produce crises, during which religion is re-examined."
(F. W. FARRAR—Critical History of Free Thought.)

"It seems to me that the mode of conceiving the operations of nature which is most widely accepted to-day, which
goes under the general designation of evolution, instead of
rendering the great cardinal truths of the gospel less credible, only renders them more credible."
(J. LEWIS DIMAN—The Theistic Argument.)

I.

INTRODUCTORY.

WHATEVER difference of opinion there may be as to the cause, there is no such difference as to the fact, of there being at the present time a general perturbation in the theological and religious thought of the world. This cannot be denied. It is too plainly seen all around, and strongly felt even within our own minds and hearts.

Not only does it show itself in the manners, methods, and utterances of the pulpit; the actions of synods and conferences; the subjects uppermost in the religious, and prominent even in the secular press, and in the tone of their treatment; the rise of "new theologies," and the multiplication of all manner of "heresies;" but especially in the general attitude of the religious public, and of the secular as reflecting that of the religious, over against the ministry, the church, and theology. There is a strong distaste for the old positive, dogmatic preaching of a few generations ago. A feeling as if there were "something the matter with it;" and on nearly the whole body of Christian doctrine an unexpressed doubtfulness, a strong tendency to decided mental reservation in the matter of its acceptance. The very dogmas which the fathers held with most intensity, the children mentally shrug their shoulders at, and at best subscribe to them only with the lips, or if they can avoid it, not even that. There is that half-heartedness, listless indifference, and yet restless expectancy of no one knows what, which are the inevitable forerunners and accompaniments of every great change in the world of thought. In a word, there is an all-pervading unsettlement, doubting, questioning, fearing; a feeling of uncertainty as to the reality of even the dearest and most precious of our faiths, and of the possibility of disappointment in even our most deeply cherished hopes.

And more than this. Among thoughtful men faith in the fundamental verities is stronger than ever. But there is a suspicion that they have been more or less hidden and covered over with much that does not essentially belong to them, and from which they ought to be freed; that much dust has settled on the walls of the temple of Truth; cobwebs have accumulated; green films of damp moss have overgrown them; and that it is time for another thorough cleansing. Everywhere men are demanding to go deeper down than the seeming, and be shown the realities. Old definitions are reinvestigated. Creeds are taken apart and criticised and reformed. Men want to go beneath them. Words, however venerable and sacred, are impatiently set aside. Things are wanted. Not the ˌvesture; the substance. Scrape off the dust, the cobwebs and moss, that we may see and verify the bare Truth itself.

If there were any proof needed of the extent and earnestness of this movement, it would be afforded us by the loud laments and fierce denunciations of those many zealous champions of that which is, who at the present time are pleading and thundering against it from hundreds of pulpits, platforms, and editorial chairs. With tears in their eyes they bewail "the degeneracy of the times." In vivid colors they paint for us the dangers and evils of what they call the prevalent spirit of rationalism, unbelief, agnosticism, and atheism. They are disconsolate over the laxity of thought and belief in the church, the spirit of insubordination, the lack of reverence for the old and established, the general defiance of ecclesiastical restraint and authority. But they fail to see or acknowledge the cause of the dreaded lapse from orthodoxy, and to read correctly its spirit or its end. Similarly are the foes of religion utterly at fault and doomed to disappointment when they loudly rejoice at the seeming disintegration of the faith, and seeing in the present movement only disagreement and confusion, boast that the downfall of divine truth is near at hand.

Neither of these unwilling witnesses seem conscious of the fact that what they deplore, and rejoice at, is but the cracking of the outer superficial shell, the proof and inevitable accompaniment of the growth and expansion of the living spirit within. "Those who defend, equally with those who assail religious creeds," says Herbert Spencer very truly, "suppose that everything turns on the maintenance of the particular dogmas at issue, whereas the dogmas are but temporary forms of that which is permanent." [1] There never yet was a forward step taken in religious thought which had not just such accompaniments as those we see around us everywhere.

And who that has read the past to any profit, who that has faith in God's providence, can doubt that the ultimate result will be only for good? The evil effects are but transitory. Their very character shows this. They are growing-pains, which are signs that the mind of man is expanding, his heart enlarging. We are moving to a higher plane of faith and of knowledge. For a time indeed we may find ourselves enveloped in mists and clouds. But this very fact is cause for greatest encouragement. It is an indication that our movement is upward. A deadlier faintness, a blacker darkness, enveloped the Truth ere now, when He struggled in Gethsemane, when He painfully mounted Calvary's heights. Aye, not till

---

[1] The Study of Sociology.

He had been lifted up on the very Cross itself did the vision become clear and men see Him to adore Him.

> " And these mounts of anguish number,
>   how each generation learned
> One new word of that grand *Credo*,
>   which in prophet-hearts hath burned,
> Since the first man stood God-conquered,
>   with his face to heaven upturned." [2]

Boldly therefore we push up their slopes, through the clouds, for we know the Light is shining undimmed beyond.

It behooves every one, surely, who has this faith, and who recognizes the full import and responsibility of his manhood, not cowardly to shirk the questions and problems presenting themselves, by the thin pretence of a mechanical profession and outward adherence to the effete symbols and forms of antiquity, or even denouncing and fighting against the various agencies that oppose them, but courageously, with firm trust in the eternal Right and Truth, to meet them, grapple with, and as far as may be, settle them. One grain of true faith, independently, honestly wrought out, even though it be small as a mustard seed, is worth more than all the truths of the catechism merely confessed with the mouth.

And, further, every thinking man owes it as a solemn duty to his fellow men to contribute

---

[2] Lowell—The Present Crisis.

his share, however small and insignificant it be, to the thought of the world and the working out of its problems.   Each individual is a unit of force in the development of humanity, and must do his part toward directing and furthering the onward movement of the universal spirit, or be untrue to himself, to mankind, and to God.   As Carlyle forcibly says, "not Mankind only, but all that Mankind does or beholds, is in continual growth, re-genesis and self-perfecting vitality. Cast forth thy Act, thy Word, into the ever-living, ever-working Universe: it is a seed-grain that cannot die." [3]

It is alone in fulfillment of this duty, and because I believe that the Truth can be found whose "Peace, be still!" shall bring a calm upon the heart of man now cruelly tossed and torn by the winds and waves of uncertainty, doubt and fear, that I have undertaken to record my thoughts on the subject and to offer them to the public in this series of Studies.

It is only a very superficial view of the present disturbance in the religious world that contents itself with attributing it to "our sinful nature," and the "depravity of the human heart."   It has other causes.   It must have. Man is not willingly an unbeliever.   His nature craves for some worthy object of belief.   And much less is he ever really an atheist from

---

[3] Sartor Resartus.

choice. Yet there are many, unusually many, of both classes so called at the present time, upright, honest, pure, and intelligent men, in the church and outside of it. They do not wish to renounce their religious beliefs, which they learned at their mothers' knees, and which there were hallowed for them. But there are so many facts forced upon them which seem directly to contradict the doctrines taught them, that they cannot believe as they once did. It would be a psychological impossibility. The most of them, probably, do not even fully accept, or understand, the antagonistic propositions; nor do they prefer to believe them rather than those of the church. But they cannot help seeing that there they are: two sets of propositions, apparently mutually contradictory, at least positively declared to be so. What are they to do? No longer seeing the Truth as one, man no longer sees the Truth at all.

Nor is it only that men are confronted with seemingly opposing facts. The harmony between the different spheres of thought has been destroyed. Outside the realm of theology the modes and methods of thinking have entirely changed. Different standards of truth are there; different words for expressing it; as it were, a wholly different atmosphere is breathed and a different light shines there. Yet instinctively the soul knows that there can be but one standard for all spheres. The double language deafens; the double atmosphere stifles; the double light blinds it. Is it a wonder then that the human spirit should struggle and cry to escape from this blackness of despair, or that its struggles should sometimes cause confusion, and its cries be incoherent? Sin and depravity would not do so; but the love of truth cannot do otherwise.

Let us endeavor, then, first of all, to discover what has brought about this disharmony. Unless we succeed in this, all efforts at restoring harmony will be in vain.

We may be guided somewhat in our task by learning from the experience of the past. Whenever a crisis like the present came, we know that it was caused either directly or indirectly by some important discovery in the realm of material nature, or the prevalence of some new theory of knowledge; that is, by some great and far-reaching change in the science or philosophy of the times. We know, too, that always the new discovery was at first denied, especially by theology, until at last it was forced reluctantly to readjust its dogmas and forms, and readapt itself to the new order of facts, laws, or modes of thought. There was a great cry of heresy and atheism when Columbus ventured to assert that there must be a hemisphere beyond the western seas. Still worse was it when Copernicus advanced the theory that the sun does not move around the earth, but the

earth and all the planets around the sun.
Theology was horrified; Copernicus hated and
hooted, cursed and persecuted. Even as late
as the end of the seventeenth century the
famous Puritan divine, the Rev. Dr. John
Owen, declared: "The late hypothesis, fixing
the sun as the center of the world, was built on
fallible phenomena, and advanced by many arbitrary presumptions against the evident testimonies of Scripture and reason." [4] There was
a revolution in theology. The pious lamented
the growth of unbelief and heresy. Their foes
boasted of the near downfall of all religion.
But finally everything was adjusted, and the
equilibrium between the religious and the scientific spheres fully restored. When Newton
discovered the law of gravitation the cry again
was everywhere raised, "It is atheism! It
denies the Bible!" The theory of Newton was
declared to be part of a deeply laid plot to
overthrow the whole theology of the Scriptures. Descartes and Kepler and Galileo were
denounced, imprisoned, and persecuted for
similar reasons.

Always there was a season of doubt, fear,
confusion in the church. But always at last its
dogmas and interpretation of the Bible, its
teachings and modes of thought, at last were
brought into harmony with the new discoveries.

---

[4] Works, vol. xix.

It seems to be a law of spiritual growth in the world that first one side, the scientific and philosophical, advances, while the other, the theological, stands still. The harmony between them is thus disturbed; their equilibrium destroyed. Violent agitation is the result, conflict and confusion. And this continues until the theological sphere makes corresponding progress, comes into harmony with the others, and thus the necessary equilibrium is restored.

To find the cause of the present unrest and agitation, therefore, we are with confidence directed to the sphere of natural science and philosophy. It must be out of harmony with the theological. Peace will only be gained by bringing them into harmony.

In the department of science we find that there have indeed been almost unprecedented advances made within the last few decades. In Astronomy, Geology, Biology, Psychology, Sociology, Comparative Theology, and indeed in almost every other science, there have been discoveries made that have overturned all previous theories, and have given rise to an entirely new conception of the universe, brought to light new facts, made necessary new methods of research, and turned the human mind into new directions and fields of knowledge. All these have ranged themselves along the line of a new system of thought, with principles more profound and comprehensive, and laws more far-reaching and universally applicable, than any known before.

Evolution is indeed still only a hypothetical theory, in the sense that it has not been fully and positively demonstrated in all its details. When we consider of how recent origin it is, and how wide the range of facts it is expected to cover, we do not wonder at this; but rather wonder that the co-ordination of laws and phenomena under it is already as complete as it is, and the acceptance of the system as general. It can only be, it appears to me, because, recognizing with Emerson that the test of the truth of a theory "is, that it will explain all phenomena," men feel that, though not yet fully proven, Evolution endures that test more satisfactorily than any other theory.

For, say what we will, the fact remains that in spite of every prejudice against it, of all the violent opposition and fierce assaults upon it, Evolution not only still exists, but is more firmly established to-day than ever before, and is steadily making its influence more and more widely felt. Everywhere thoughtful men are being deeply affected by such fundamental facts as the correlation and conservation of force, the antiquity of the earth and of man, the influence of heredity, natural selection, and those laws brought to light by the new science of sociology. And although they do not by any means all agree as to details, yet as to the general principle of Evolution there is evidently enough truth in it to have already won over to it most of the leading men of science, not a few prominent theologians even, and to have influenced to a really remarkable degree the whole current of popular thought and belief. It is the reigning philosophy. It holds full sway in the physical sciences. Art has been sensibly affected by it. Its phraseology at least is fashionable in literature. The very text-books of our public schools use its language and imply its principles. Its friends, its foes, and the indifferent alike must confess with the late eminent thinker, Dr. J. Lewis Diman, that "the doctrine of evolution may be said to sum up and comprehend the speculative movement of our time. It is the word which science pronounces as a solution of the riddle of existence, the characteristic form in which the thought of the present age has shaped itself. . . . This doctrine must be accepted then as the characteristic note of contemporary thought." [5]

Now all the prevalent disturbance and uneasiness in the theological and religious world are simply the result of the recognition that it is not in accord with this "characteristic note of contemporary thought," that the equilibrium of the thought-world has been disturbed; and

---

[5] The Theistic Argument.

then the striving of some to bring it into more
or less complete accord, and the refusal of
others to do anything of the kind.

It is the former tendency that is so strongly
felt in the department of Biblical criticism, for
instance, represented by Wellhausen, Kuenen,
Robertson Smith and others, in Europe, and
numbers of their followers in this country. The
whole "new movement" in theology, that has
started in New England, is but another phase of
this same tendency, embracing leading men under it, in the foremost ranks of probably all de-
nominations. I am well aware that many of
these very men are openly opposed to the philosophy of Evolution as a whole. The most of
them are probably not aware of its influence as
the ultimate ground of their discontent with the
old; nor of the reason, lying deep down beneath all others, which gives the particular
direction to their thought and endeavors. I
cannot but regard this as unfortunate. For all
reform and revision that does not recognize the
principle underlying it, and in obedience to
which alone it can succeed, must involve a great
deal of waste of time and energy. Far better
would it be were the root of the whole matter
at once fairly and clearly acknowledged, and
then the efforts of all united in the one definite
direction. Yet even as it is, a good work is
being done by this movement, which, though
more or less disjointed and indefinite, is on the

whole helping mightily to bring about the desired result, and to reach the true end, of which many of the workers may themselves not be clearly conscious.

All the more earnestly, therefore, let those who do recognize the real cause of the present disturbance in thought to be the vague, half-unconscious feeling of a discord between theology on the one hand, and nearly all the rest of the departments of knowledge and belief on the other, aim directly at the removal of this cause. Bring them into harmony. Whatever diversity there may be between their several forms and modes of thought and expression, there is nothing in the essential principles of Evolution, as I hope to succeed in showing, that contradicts any of the essential facts of the Christian religion. I lay stress upon the word *essential* here. For there are current many different theories built up of materialistic and atheistic interpretations, and inferences which are not necessarily nor legitimately involved in the fundamental principles themselves. With them we have nothing to do.

As defined by Herbert Spencer, Evolution "is an integration of matter and concomitant dissipation of motion; during which the matter passes from an indefinite, incoherent homogeneity to a definite, coherent heterogeneity, and during which the retained motion under goes a parallel transformation."* Without entering here upon the question whether this is an adequate and sufficiently comprehensive definition or not, it is enough for us to learn from it that all that evolutionists intend is to give us a generalized statement of the process according to which the various phenomena of the world advance from simple and lower to more complicated and higher conditions and forms of being, verifiable by observed facts and experiments. Now when we remember that the Bible and religion tell us nothing at all about methods, how can Evolution contradict or in any way come in conflict with them, since it tells us as little about anything else but methods?

But further than this, I hope to show that the fundamental principles of Evolution in so far positively sustain those of the Christian religion, and make them more easily intelligible. I believe, for example, that correctly and consistently interpreted they will help us to truer and loftier conceptions of the being and nature of God than we had before. Their influence in this direction is already being felt and acknowledged in the more recent works on theology. So likewise they directly substantiate and explain such Scripture teachings as the unity of the race, the innate sinfulness of man,

---

* First Principles.

and indeed all the other fundamental doctrines
of our religion.

Of course, I do not maintain that Evolution
will agree with every detail of our present systems of theology, nor with some of the popular
interpretations of passages of Scripture. But I
do hold that all that is essential in the theory
will be found reconcilable with the vital, essential facts of Christianity. There may have
to be, nay, there will be, changes in the accepted views of what the Bible says, just as
there have often been such changes before; but
only on points not affecting the spiritual truths
of religion. There was a time when the Bible
was thought to teach that the earth was flat,
shaped like a plate. Science discovered its
spherical form, and though it was denounced as
contrary to Scripture, the truth yet prevailed;
and then, on closer examination, it was found
that the Bible had never taught anything
different. Man's interpretation had been wrong,
that was all; not the Bible. So it was long
confidently believed that Revelation taught that
the sun moved around the earth. But it never
taught anything of the kind; men had only
read it wrongly. It was until comparatively
recent times that people imagined that the
Bible declared the earth to have been created in
six days of twenty-four hours each. Geology
showed that this must be a mistake; and, sure
enough, on looking more closely it appeared that

man's interpretation had again been incorrect, and that the Bible said nothing about the duration of the work of creation. Yet after all these changes in human exegesis, true religion was as strong, and stronger, than it had been before.

There is, therefore, nothing alarming in the prospect that we may possibly have to make some further corrections in our ideas of what Revelation declares to us. We hail such changes if they shall lead us to a fuller, clearer view of the divine Truth. We are not conceited enough to imagine, I trust, that we have already attained to all knowledge and wisdom; but humble enough to believe that we may have made some more mistakes in our Scripture interpretation, and that there may be yet undreamed-of gems of richest truth in the Word of God reserved for our future instruction and enlightenment. The more mistakes of ours are found out, the more clearly will God's truth appear; and the fuller the measure of truth we enjoy, the purer and loftier will be our religion.

There has been and must still be growth, development, progress towards perfection, in our knowledge of God as well as in everything else. "No more in this than in other things," to use the language of Mr. Spencer, "will evolution alter its general direction: it will continue along the same lines as hitherto."' For

---

' The Study of Sociology.

every old and false notion we may have to surrender, we will be compensated by the reception
of a multitude of truer, better facts. It has
ever been thus; and thus ever it will be.

In the sphere of systematic theology there have
been vast changes in the past, even in recent
times; and they are still going on. As the
British laureate beautifully puts it:

> " Our little systems have their day;
> 　　They have their day and cease to be;
> 　　They are but broken lights of thee,
> And thou, O Lord, art more than they." [8]

Yes, for thou, O Lord, art the Truth himself,
and they are but feeble human gropings after
thee, if haply they may feel after and find
thee! How have our views and definitions of
God changed, been purified, since the days of
scholasticism, or even since the times of early
Puritanism! The doctrine of the atonement
is to-day held in a far different form from the
harsh and repellant conceptions of a few centuries ago. Not less has been the advance
through change in the doctrines of sin, regeneration, the divine justice, and others just as
fundamental, since the Rev. Michael Wiggles-
worth, A. M., embodied the popular theology of
his times in his "Day of Doom," verses which,
according to Prof. Moses Coit Tyler, had a
"popular influence only inferior to that of the

---

[8] In Memoriam.

Bible and the Shorter Catechism;" ' in which, among much that is even worse, God is represented as thus replying to the unbaptized infants who plead for mercy at his judgment bar:

"Am I alone of what's my own no master or no Lord?
Or if I am, how can you claim what I to some afford?
Will you demand Grace at my hand, and challenge what is
    mine?
Will you teach me whom to set free, and thus my Grace
    confine?

"You sinners are, and such a share as sinners may expect,
Such you shall have; for I do save none but my own Elect.
Yet to compare your sin with theirs who liv'd a longer time
I do confess yours is much less, though every sin's a crime.

"A Crime it is, therefore in bliss you may not hope to dwell;
But unto you I shall allow the easiest room in Hell.
The glorious King thus answering they cease and plead no
    longer:
Their Consciences must needs confess his Reasons are the
    stronger." [10]

Shall we then arrogantly suppose that in our day all growth has suddenly stopped? We cannot. For not only is it even now mightily going on all around us, but it must go on. It is the very nature of all truth to do so. As Dr. T. T. Munger truly says, "It is a mistake to regard the truths of the Christian faith, even those that are called leading and fundamental, as having a fixed form. . . . Truth is not something handed down from heaven, a moral

---

[9] History of American Literature.
[10] Quoted by Tyler, *supra*.

parcel of known size and weight, but is a dis-
closure of God through the order of the world
and of the Spirit." [11]

We may therefore as well expect at the out-
set, and without being in the least alarmed
thereat, that there will have to be some considerable changes in our present systems of
theology, and forms and habits of theological
thought, before anything like a proper equilibrium in the spiritual world will be reached.
Schleiermacher's "presentiment" may even
have to be fulfilled, of which he wrote as early
as 1829 to a younger friend, "that we will yet
have to learn to do without a great deal which
many still are accustomed to think is inextri-
cably involved in the very essence of Christianity." But I firmly believe that every change
that will be made and confirmed will be only
for the better. "Like the transformations that
have succeeded one another hitherto," again to
quote Mr. Spencer, "the transformation now in
progress is but an advance from a lower form,
no longer fit, to a higher and fitter form; and
neither will this transformation, nor kindred
transformations to come hereafter, destroy that
which is transformed more than past transformations have destroyed it." [12]

On the contrary, I confidently maintain and
hope to be able to prove, that the influence of

----

[11] The Freedom of Faith.
[12] The Study of Sociology.

Evolution, so far as it bears on the subject, will not only not weaken, but greatly strengthen and enlighten, our living, practical religious faith in an all-wise and ever-present, omnipotent, all-loving Father. Our belief in immortality will not suffer by having demonstrated to it the absolute indestructibility of all entities. Our trust in Providence, confidence in the use of prayer, and solemn sense of personal responsibility, will not be made feebler, though they may be deepened, broadened, and made more intelligent, by being shown how unalterably fixed are the eternal laws according to which all things subsist, from the merest mote that flies in the air, to the most intricate thought or feeling in the heart of man, or the sentiments and deeds of a heterogeneous crowd, community, or race. Nor will our deep consciousness of sinfulness and longing for salvation be enfeebled by being instructed as to the influence of the laws of heredity, reversal to type, and the relations between organism and environment.

We may, indeed, have to realize how much of truth there is in Carlyle's saying, that "First must the dead Letter of Religion own itself dead, and drop piecemeal into dust, if the living Spirit of Religion, freed from this its charnel-house, is to arise on us, new-born of heaven, and with new healing under its wings." [13] But

---

[13] Sartor Resartus.

2

even while losing much of the old shell of formal theology, the devout Christian need surrender none of the life of his Christianity; none of his faith in the redeeming, saving power of the great Spirit of Right, Truth, self-sacrificing Love, of Holiness, that Eternal Word who for a time was concretely embodied in the flesh, that we might behold his glory, and thence forward forever live only his life, the only true Man's life;—none of his love to his fellow men, his sympathy and helpfulness; none of his hope in that future when good shall have conquered evil, and there shall be no more tears nor sickness, no sin, and no more night of ignorance there, but he who is Love shall be all and in all, and shall fill heaven and earth with his glory. This faith, this love, this hope, no theology can give and no philosophy can take away. This religion Evolution helps us to hold and encourages us to practice.

For, whatever may be the outcome of the present tendency as regards the contents of men's belief, its effects on the spirit of religion must be decidedly salutary. Already thoughtful men, spurred on by the very doubt that prevails, and the feeling of impatience of every restraint and authority in spiritual matters, are everywhere engaged in earnest, independent thought, research, and study. This is in itself a guarantee of good things to come.

It is not till we have ourselves labored, struggled, and perhaps suffered for our faith in the process of making it a part of our being, that it becomes a personal, living, working conviction in us. One single fact thus obtained is worth more than a thousand merely passively accepted. Truth received at second hand is indeed better than none at all, as reflected light is better than darkness. But at best how different it is from the living flame itself, shining direct and immediate into our very soul! What a glow and living warmth it infuses, such as the feeble reflection scarce gave us a hint of! We no longer only look at it and admire. It fills us, takes possession, becomes part of ourselves, or rather makes us part of itself. We not only see it. It touches us all over. We not only believe it. We have it; we absorb, we live it. It becomes a vital, working force in our lives, beside which a dozen creeds given us from without by another seem but as a tale that is told. They may be far more elaborate, far more complete than it, as infinitely superior as is some grand old domed cathedral to a backwoods hut of logs. But the hut is mine! I have built it. I know every log, every stone in it. It is my *home*. It is to me what all the cathedrals in the world could never be.

If nothing more were gained than this, the vivifying and re-invigorating of our practical religiousness, it would be worth all that it will cost. And that my humble efforts to guide and assist my fellow men in attaining to such a state, by removing the doubt and uncertainty that now prevent it, and showing them at least in what direction peace and strength-giving harmony are to be sought between the several departments of truth that seem to be at present engaged in an unnatural warfare;—that a sense of the unity of all truth, the agreement and cooperation of all its parts, making for the everlasting glory of God, a certainty as deep, as satisfying, and as inspiring as that which through these studies I have reached, may also fill their souls to the realization of that peace of God which passeth understanding,—this is my most earnest prayer; and if it shall be fulfilled even only in part, this shall be my greatest satisfaction and cause for sincerest thanksgiving to him, the divine Spirit of God, who alone can guide us into all truth.

II.

GOD.

"In him we live and move and have our being."

PAUL—*Acts* 17: 28.

" Man cannot be God's outlaw if he would,
  Nor so abscond him in the caves of sense
  But Nature still shall search some crevice out
  With messages of splendor from that Source
  Which, dive he, soar he, baffles still and lures."

(LOWELL—*The Cathedral.*)

"The fiction of an unknown or distant or sleeping
divinity has completely disappeared, and the Living God
of science brightens the whole universe."

(KESHUB CHUNDER SEN, in the *Independent.*)

" Was wär' ein Gott, der nur von aussen stiesse,
  Im Kreis das All am Finger laufen liesse!
  Ihm ziemts die Welt im Innern zu bewegen,
  Natur in Sich, Sich in Natur zu hegen;
  So dass, was in Ihm lebt und webt und ist,
  Nie seine Kraft, nie seinen Geist vermisst."

(GOETHE—*Sprüche in Reimen.*)

" It is the characteristic thought of God at present that
He is immanent in all created things,—immanent yet personal, the life of all lives, the power of all powers, the soul
of the universe; that He is most present where there is most
perfection."

(T. T. MUNGER—*The Freedom of Faith.*)

" When we have broken our god of tradition, and ceased
from our god of rhetoric, then may God fire the heart with
his presence."

(EMERSON—*The Over-Soul.*)

II.

GOD.

If we may judge from the frequency with which we hear and read the word "atheist" nowadays, the world must be full of fools. For nothing is more certain than that the Psalmist was correct when he declared, "The fool hath said in his heart, there is no God."

And yet we know that there are many men, more at the present time, perhaps, than ever before, who have said "There is no God," and who nevertheless are not fools. Some of them indeed are worse. They have affirmed with their lips what in their hearts they knew to be untrue,—probably for the sake of notoriety, or even only in order to make money by their dishonest, blasphemous lectures. Others have said it who were simply mistaken as to their own convictions, or incorrect in their expression. They did not really mean that there is no God; but that there is no such God as is represented by this or that teacher. The evil is not theirs so much as that of those who by their false and narrow definitions of God have rendered belief in him impossible to many; and by their dogmatic positiveness have made the popular impression that unless their notion and definition be accepted, atheism is the only possible alternative.

These are the ones who by their lavish application of the term atheist would people all the world outside of themselves with fools, thereby committing the greatest folly of all. Socrates was denounced as an atheist, and killed for it, because he did not believe in the gods pictured and worshiped by the Athenians. Yet he did believe in God, and his faith was more correct and noble far than that of his judges and murderers. They, and not he, were the worse atheists and fools. And since his time there have been not a few like him and like them in this respect. Some of the best and wisest men of our time have been called atheists, when in reality they were far more devout and true believers than those who thus slandered them. "If we must be as these are," they have exclaimed, "then much rather will we do without faith and without religion." And the recoil from the positiveness and arrogant presumption of their accusers has driven them further into agnosticism or indifference than ever they would otherwise have gone, or than calm consistency with their principles warranted.

Though there is a more temperate class, and it is steadily growing in influence and numbers, the mass of men is still divided between these two antagonistic parties. And as the one con-

sists mainly of those who profess to be evolutionists, and those who, without professing it
have yet had their thoughts largely moulded by
the all-pervading influence of the philosophy of
Evolution, while the other is composed of the
open opponents of this theory and professed
believers in the Bible and the Christian religion,
it naturally is made to appear that Evolution
and Christianity are directly contradictory of
each other as far as their teachings on the being
and nature of God are concerned. Indeed on
no other subject is the prevalent lack of harmony in human thought more apparent. Nowhere is the equilibrium more visibly and
violently disturbed. Yet it is probably nowhere
more superficial and groundless than just here.

For, there is absolutely nothing in the fundamental principles of Evolution, on the one
hand, to necessitate the total agnosticism professed by some of its adherents, nor of Christianity on the other to warrant the expressions
of minute and presumptuous knowledge in-
dulged in by the orthodox. The Bible does not
tell us nearly as much about the divine being
and nature as some of the still current theology does; and Evolution implies more about
them than some evolutionists say it does, and
than it is popularly credited with. If the mistakes of both were corrected, there would result
a conception of God, different indeed from
many that are current, but only because far

clearer, truer, more lofty and ennobling. This will, however, never be accomplished by mutual fear, hatred, abuse and denunciation; but only by an honest attempt at mutual understanding of each other's principles, and then a fair mutual adaptation and adjustment of forms of thought and expression.

The truth of the Bible and the truth of Evolution are one. The only conflict is between its several interpreters and exponents. Make the world realize this, and true religion will no longer be hampered and hindered by enervating doubt and degrading suspicion, hatred and strife; but will again exert its beneficent power in the prosecution of its legitimate and most blessed work.

Let us do our humble part in bringing this about, by trying to show, first, that atheism and materialism are forever rendered impossible by Evolution; then, that Evolution is inconsistent with agnosticism; and finally, that in the true God, the God of the Bible and of nature, the God to whom the intelligence and heart of man freely, sincerely, joyously go out in loving worship, the evolutionist and the Christian can alike believe.

Absolute atheism is a logical impossibility to the consistent evolutionist. Hence while we find very few even of the leaders in this philosophy who are perfectly consistent in everything, in this nearly all of them are, that they hold to

the existence of a supra-sensuous Being, distinct
from and greater than the phenomena of the
universe, and indeed the ultimate cause of them
all.   By it have the glories of our present
siderial system been slowly evolved from a
mass of vague homogeneous vapor, scattered
throughout the trackless expanse of space.   By
it this originally formless cloud was first broken
up into parts, through the secondary agency of
the various modes of gravitation, which brought
together two or more of its atoms, which again
became the nuclei of larger clusters, until these
at length gained a certain definiteness and in-
dependence, and at last, by virtue of their ac-
quired rotary motion, became the globes, with
definite orbits and coherent arrangement, that
we now consider their normal condition.   The
gases of the earth, after being detached from
their parent mass, condensed, forming a fiery
liquid nucleus; over which again in time a solid
crust was developed, and after the lapse of ages
was arranged in the different layers and strata
with which we are acquainted.   Then came the
evolution of life, by the action of the same
ultimate Power, from the lowest forms of organic being, through various stages, up to the
lords of creation.   And parallel with this was
the development of mind; and the further
differentiation of man into families, tribes,
nations, and races; and the growth of religion, society, government, and the various oc-

cupations of man, as they exist now, and still are growing.

Evolution thus simply attempts to tell us *how* "God created the heavens and the earth," and *how* "without him was not anything made that was made," of which the Bible merely states the fact *that*. Yet for doing this it is declared to be atheistic! The only reason seems to be that strange perversity of the human mind described by Frances Power Cobbe when she said, "It is a singular fact that, whenever we find out how anything is done, our first conclusion seems to be that God did not do it. No matter how wonderful, how beautiful, how infinitely complex and delicate has been the machinery which has worked, perhaps for centuries, perhaps for millions of ages, to bring about some beneficent result,—if we can but catch a glimpse of the wheels, its divine character disappears. The machinery did it all. It would be altogether superfluous to look further." [1]

Far from giving any sanction to such a groundless notion, the doctrine of Evolution demands the existence of God as a fundamental postulate, as the chief corner-stone of the entire system. We may say it is as essential to Evolution as it is to Christianity. And Herbert Spencer realizes this to the full; one might almost think more fully than certain Christian

---

[1] Darwinism in Morals.

philosophers and theologians in the past have
done. For, too many of them had rather
weakened than otherwise the validity and authority of man's belief in God by making it
the declaration of a special faculty of the mind,
the "faith faculty," as Max Müller calls it,
which had a different kind of authority from
that of the other mental powers; a mere "inspired belief," or a "revelation," as Sir Wm.
Hamilton thought it to be, to be held as it
were in defiance of the laws of our mind.

Mr. Spencer, on the contrary, makes our belief to be of equal reality and validity with any
other declaration of the soul. He endeavors
to "show that this fundamental cognition is
neither, as the idealist asserts, an illusion, nor
as the skeptic thinks, of doubtful worth, nor as
is held by the natural realist, an inexplicable
intuition; but that it is a legitimate deliverance
of consciousness, elaborating its materials after
the laws of its normal action." It "has a
higher warrant than any other whatever." [2]
Just as we have a right to believe our eyes, or
ears, or our reason when it tells us that two
and two make four, that a straight line is the
shortest distance between two points, or that
every effect must have a cause, so we have the
same right to believe our consciousness when it
tells us there must be a God. This Mr. Spen-

---

[2] First Principles.

cer declares in the most convincing manner,
insisting on it as a fact "deeper than demonstration, deeper even than definite cognition,
deep as the very nature of the mind. Its authority transcends all other whatever." [s] And
nearly all prominent evolutionists in so far fully
agree with him. It is therefore simple ignorance, where it is not worse, to maintain that
Evolution involves atheism. It does just the
opposite. In as far as the existence of God is
capable of proof, it furnishes such proof more
fully and convincingly than has ever been done
before.

And the very principles on which it proceeds
in doing this, also render any materialistic conceptions of God utterly impossible.

The ultimate basis upon which the entire
system of Evolution is built, is that most wonderful and important of all discoveries since the
fact of gravitation flashed upon Newton's mind,
the law of the Correlation and Conservation of
Forces, or more briefly, of the Persistence of
Force.

Just as not an atom of matter is ever lost or
destroyed, but ever the absolute quantity in
the universe remains the same, so according to
this law not a particle of force is annihilated.
It undergoes different changes of form and
manifestation, but not an ounce of it is ever lost

---

[s] First Principles.

or disappears. Light, electricity, gravitation, heat, and all other forces, are only so many different manifestations of one substance or entity behind them all, and the sum of them all; just as rain, clouds, dew, rivers, the billows of the ocean, are but so many different forms of the one substance water. You can change heat into electricity, or into light, but you only change the form of the substance, not the substance itself, which always remains undiminished and the same; it persists in spite of and through all change. In the language of Spencer, "The manifestations, as occurring in ourselves or outside of us, do not persist; but that which persists in the unknown cause of these manifestations." ' This is the "Ultimate Reality," the "Absolute Being," the "Great First Cause," by whom all things are and in whom all consist, the same yesterday, to-day, and forevermore, which Evolution posits at the very beginning of all knowledge, and of which Revelation declares, "In the beginning God."

It goes without saying that this Being cannot be material. No material substance, as we know materiality, would in any wise answer the conditions of its existence. We know it expressly only as distinct and different from matter. It is invisible, intangible, imponderable, and without dimensions. We can think of

---

' First Principles.

it only as immaterial, and hence, in so far, as spirit. It is God. No wonder that the late Dr. Youmans, who was one of the most uncompromising evolutionists, exclaims that, through the law of the Persistence of Force, "from the baldest materiality we rise at last to a truth of the spiritual world, of so exalted an order that it has been said 'to connect the mind of man with the spirit of God;'" [5] while Dr. Mayer, the German discoverer of the law, declares explicitly that "there are three categories of existence, matter, force, and the soul or spiritual principle." [6] Mr. Spencer even, while refusing to posit or deny anything whatever of the First Cause, is yet forced to confess that, "were we compelled to choose between the alternatives [of speaking of it in terms of matter or of spirit], the latter alternative would seem the more acceptable of the two." [7] And Prof. Fiske, Spencer's most earnest and able exponent in this country, declares that "we may say that God is Spirit, though we may not say, in the materialistic sense, that God is Force." [8] Even Prof. Huxley implies the same when he says that "the materialistic position that there is nothing in the world but matter, force, and

---

[5] The Correlation and Conservation of Forces.

[6] Discourse at the Scientific Reunion at Innsbruck.

[7] Principles of Psychology, vol. i.

[8] Outlines of Cosmic Philosophy, vol. ii. Cf. The Idea of God—Preface.

necessity, is as utterly devoid of justification as
the most baseless of theological dogmas,"[9]
though on this point, as indeed on others too,
he sometimes flatly contradicts himself, and
might also be quoted to the opposite effect.
Nevertheless, the great bulk of the most prominent evolutionists openly disavow materialism;
while even of those who do not, who boldly
profess materialism, as some do, there are few
whom consistency does not often betray into language that is irreconcilable with their profession.

Indeed so deeply is the inadequacy of matter
to account for the various phenomena and laws
of nature felt to be, that in order to retain the
name even, materialists have had to re-define it.
So that even when they speak of it, they mean
something that has none of the qualities and
attributes of matter as ordinarily understood,
but that comes as near as possible to what spirit
is commonly supposed to be. We may therefore unqualifiedly accept the acknowledgment
of Prof. Fiske, that "One grand result of the
enormous progress achieved during the past
forty years in the analysis of both physical and
psychical phenomena has been the final and
irretrievable overthrow of the materialistic hypothesis."[10]

That this "irretrievable overthrow" cannot
be restricted in its influence to the sphere of

---

[9] Lay Sermons.
[10] Cosmic Philosophy, vol. ii.

natural science and philosophy, but must also extend into that of our popular theology, is cause for deepest gratification. For nowhere were the harmful effects of materialistic conceptions of spiritual facts more sorely felt than there. The long-current "carpenter theory" of God and the universe has received its death-blow; and with it, we trust, all that formal, mechanical, lifeless ecclesiasticism that too long usurped the place of a living, working, genuine soul-religion.

No man could feel himself vitally interested in, and intimately related to, a God who sat high in the far-off heavens; who, having created the world by his fiat, wound it up and set it going, then retired into himself, and deigned only from an infinite distance to rule and govern his handiwork. Nor could rational and moral beings truly love and adore a celestial Ruler who, by the materialistic anthropomorphism that was current in the minds of the masses, was represented almost identically as we represent some earthly potentate, only vaster, more gigantic; seated on a white throne, with a crown on his head and scepter in his right hand; whose whole anatomy, as it were, formal theology mapped out for us, and whose psychology it explained as minutely as that of a man, describing his thoughts, his change of mind, his feelings and motives, and professing to tell how he could be roused to anger, soothed

and persuaded, pleased and gratified, just as
though he were some earthly magnate.

It is true, thoughtful men never soberly held
such views. They held to the spiritual teachings of the Bible, not only to its letter. They
knew that these sought to impress upon man as
emphatically and clearly as language can, the
grand fact that "God is a Spirit," and as such
is in intimate and continuous union and communion with man. He is never far away, but
ever near at hand; never only there, but ever
here. He is with us alway, even to the end of
the world; and in him we live, and move, and
have our being.

But in the popular mind this truth was, and
still is, too commonly lost sight of. The sym-
bolic language of the Scriptures and the pulpit
was taken literally. It could scarcely be otherwise. Man thinks by comparison and analogy.
But so long as he knew of nothing anywhere
according to which he could fashion his ideas
of spirit, except the mind of man, of creation
except the work of a mechanic, of government
except the rule of a monarch, not to say tyrant,
and of love except the subjective feelings and
impulses of his own heart, it was well nigh
impossible for him to think of God otherwise
than as a large man, only less symmetrical,
more unnatural.

It is the great merit of Evolution, however,
now to have given us the means of realizing

God in a manner more worthy of his infinite
and absolute being, freed from the limitations
of time and space to a degree not possible before. Nay, it has done more. It enables us to
a certain extent to apprehend God's essential
self, without the need of pictures, symbols, and
representations, and to understand more fully
than ever before, his methods and modes of
being and action, the exercise of his power, the
manner of his government, the nature of his
love. The law of the Persistence of Force
brings us face to face with him, the Spirit-
power, "without whom was not anything
made that was made," immanent in the whole
universe and in every minutest atom of the
same. We can no longer think of him as far
away; for it is literally and really his whisper
we hear in the tree tops, his radiance that flows
a golden stream of light from the sun, his breath
that drives the clouds, like a snowy flock before
their shepherd, through the pastures of the
sky.

> " Thy voice is on the rolling air;
>   I hear thee where the waters run;
>   Thou standest in the rising sun,
> And in the setting thou art fair.

> " Far off thou art, but ever nigh;
>   I have thee still, and I rejoice:
>   I prosper circled with thy voice;
>   I shall not lose thee, though I die." [11]

---

[11] Tennyson—In Memoriam.

Forces of nature? It is a misnomer. They are all the emanations of the one Power; and that one is God, in however infinite a variety of rays and beams he shines. Laws of nature? There is but one; and that one is God himself living out the eternal order of his being. Whether it be gravitation, light, heat, electricity; whether it be in the vast might that forms the suns and planets, and floats them through the firmament, or the more exquisite power that fashions the crystals of the snow-flake and gently drifts their starry host down through the air;—everywhere, near and far, in everything, Evolution shows us God, directly and palpably present. We no longer ask for nor need any feeble definitions of him. We see him. We feel him. We live him. Undefinable because like only to himself; incomprehensible because himself comprehending all things.

> " He is the axis of the star;
> He is the sparkle of the spar;
> He is the heart of every creature;
> He is the meaning of each feature;
> And his mind is the sky,
> Than all it holds more deep, more high." [19]

From the foregoing it will already have appeared that the very principles of Evolution preclude that total agnosticism with which it is charged, and which many of its adherents profess. I maintain that, where Mr. Spencer,

---

[19] Emerson—Woodnotes.

Professors Huxley, Tyndal, the late Mr. Darwin and others, repeatedly declare that we can know nothing further of the Ultimate Reality than that it exists, they are manifestly inconsistent, so manifestly that it seems inexplicable that they themselves should not have discovered and corrected their mistake. They all speak of the "Great Unknown," and the "absolutely Inscrutable," and even of the "Unknown Cause." Yet so incompatible is agnosticism with their own fundamental principles that they all repeatedly show themselves better than their profession, and ascribe various attributes to the Unknown. Thus showing that Evolution is more consistent than any individual evolutionist.

In the first place, Mr. Spencer, when speaking for his system and elaborating its laws, over and over again declares his Great Unknown to be known as a cause, the "First Cause" of everything that is. Indeed this is involved in the very corner-stone of his whole system, the principle of the Persistence of Force. The real Substance that persists beneath and behind all appearances is known to us as a cause, or not at all. We know it not otherwise than as a cause existing. Hence, surely, so far at least it is not unknown, but very positively known.

But Mr. Spencer himself goes still further. As if to leave no doubt in our minds that this First Cause is he of whom Revelation says, "In

the beginning God created the heaven and the
earth," he proceeds to define it [13] as "Absolute
Being," as a power "which must be in every
sense perfect, complete, total," and "including
within itself all power, and transcending all
law." This is in fact so necessarily implied in
the law mentioned before, that Mr. Spencer
could not but acknowledge it. Nor can or does
he deny this almighty Being the further divine
attributes of eternity and omnipresence. For
they are inevitably involved in the Ultimate
Reality, of which, as he says, [14] "neither begin-
ing nor end can be conceived," and which must
be thought of as omnipresent, because "though
omnipresence is unthinkable, yet, as experience
discloses no bounds to the diffusion of phenomena, we are unable to think of limits to the
presence of this power" that is the cause of
them all, that is

> " All things, and yet no Thing,
> The fair and the unfair;
> He has nor foot, nor wing,
> And yet is everywhere."

"Whither shall I go from thy Spirit? or whither
shall I flee from thy presence? If I ascend up
into heaven, thou art there: if I make my bed
in hell, behold, thou art there. If I take the
wings of the morning, and dwell in the utter-

---

[13] First Principles.
[14] Ibid.

most parts of the sea; even there shall thy hand lead me, and thy right hand shall hold me. If I say, Surely the darkness shall cover me; even the night shall be light about me. Yea, the darkness hideth not from thee: but the night shineth as the day: the darkness and the light are both alike to thee."

What, therefore, the principles of Evolution are admitted to teach by the founders of that philosophy themselves, is in so far in the most intimate agreement with the doctrines of revealed religion. They both declare the existence of a Supreme Being, who is not material; both teach that he made all things, and is ever active in sustaining them; that he is infinite and absolute, almighty, omnipresent, and eternal. So far the only difference between the two is a difference of names. The one calls the Absolute Being God, the other calls him the Great Unknown. Surely scarce a difference worth quarrelling about. For whatever his name, the ultimate reality remains; both mean the same divine Being; not unknown, but only uncomprehended; not fully known, but yet apprehended. Both can worship him in Lowell's words,

> " O Power, more near my life than life itself
> (Or what seems life to us in sense immured),
> Even as the roots, shut in the darksome earth,
> Share in the tree-top's joyance, and conceive
> Of sunshine and wide air and winged things
> By sympathy of nature, so do I

Have evidence of thee so far above
Yet in and of me. Rather thou the root
Invisibly sustaining, hid in light,
Not darkness, or in darkness made by us." [16]

Further than this, while the teachings of our religion declare that God made the world, a statement over which the feeble mind of man long was perplexed, being unable to realize it, Evolution throws a stream of light upon it by saying, Yes, he made it, by operating thus through gravitation, so through heat, and thus through the different chemical forces; through the same agencies, and according to the same order of development, that we now see going on in the realms of astronomy, the depths of stellar space; of geology, in the bowels of the earth; of botany, in every field and forest around us; and of physiology, in the department of animal life without us and within. Not by finite means such as man must use, nor with hands and feet, feeble tools and instruments; but in ways more worthy of an unconditioned and unlimited Being, and according to a method more divine by far.

Even if we should not agree with these statements, we surely cannot say that they deny or contradict our religion. As little as Evolution is atheistic, so little is it agnostic as far as these are concerned. This is so very evident that I cannot think that a man like Herbert Spencer

---

[16] The Cathedral.

should not have seen it. When he so strenuously affirms that we can know nothing whatever about the First Cause, he must use the words "know" and "knowledge" in the limited sense in which he often employs them as applying only to what is positively definable, with mathematical precision, and to what can be pictured to the mind adequately, immediately, without the aid of any symbols of thought, in other words, what is fully comprehensible.[16] In this sense, of course, we cannot know God. And whatever some theologians may have done, the Bible certainly never claimed such knowledge for man, but continually reminds him that God's ways are not our ways, that no man can by searching find him out, that the finite can never hope to comprehend the infinite; so that none of its names and comparisons are ever to be taken as adequate descriptions, and none of its symbolical terms and phrases as literal representations or exhaustive explanations. All too commonly, however, has this been utterly disregarded, to the degradation of true religion, the generation of unbelief and scorn, and the mighty encouragement of agnosticism and atheism.

Let us bear this in mind especially in our further inquiries into the nature of the divine Being. For the human heart cannot rest con-

---

[16] Cf. Fiske—The Idea of God—Preface.

tent with those attributes of God we have
already found. They alone would do no more
than lead it into the ever-disappointing, finally
fatal, quicksands of pantheism. As a late theologian, from whom I have quoted before, says,
" If I cannot connect it (the first cause) with
intelligence and with personality, we have not
advanced a step in satisfying the demands of
religion;" " but not with human intelligence
and personality.

Just here, in the attempt to make this connection, has been the cause of all the idolatry
and ideolatry, the many superstitions and materialistic forms of anthropomorphism, that have
in the past so often stifled true religion. And
it is probably therefore that not only Mr. Spencer, Matthew Arnold, and such as they, but
many devout theologians as well, have persistently shrunk from attributing personality to
God. From the current conceptions of personality I shrink as much as they. I as earnestly
deplore the impiety of ascribing to God an intelligence and will, feelings, purposes, thoughts,
and motives such as are the results of human
limitations, and are totally incompatible with
the idea of absolute and infinite Being. I
would not for a moment venture the presumptuous thought that God is a person merely as we
are persons. And in using the word, I do so

---

[17] Diman—The Theistic Argument.

only because I do not find any other term by
which we could better express an essential fact
that necessarily enters into our conception of
God; a fact which we cannot define or explain
even to ourselves, and of which the expression
in words must therefore be only very partial
and inadequate; but a fact of which as a fact
we are as certain and sure as of any other contained in human consciousness, and which is
not contradicted but rather sustained by Evolution.

As applying to man we may accept either or
both of the two latest and best definitions of
personality offered. According to Dr. Geo.
P. Fisher, "The essential characteristics of personality are self-consciousness and self-deter-
mination," [18] which Dr. Samuel Harris narrows
down a little, so that he thinks "A person is a
being conscious of self, subsisting in individu-
ality and identity, and endowed with intuitive
reason, rational sensibility and free-will." [19]
The consistent evolutionist would, however,
probably hesitate to apply either of these unqualifiedly to God. And I too recognize with
Mr. Spencer not only the possibility of "a mode
of being as much transcending intelligence and
will as these transcend mechanical motion,"
but the necessity of regarding the divine, from
what we already know of it, as such a mode of

---

[18] The Grounds of Theistic and Christian Belief.
[19] The Philosophical Basis of Theism.

being. All that we are warranted in affirming
of it, and which, I think, will be deemed fully
satisfactory to the humble heart, is this:
Though we can discern no apparent likeness
between God's nature and man's because the
two are incapable of comparison, we can and
do discern a likeness between his and our
acts in their results. When I am conscious,
for example, in lifting a stone, of exerting force by an exercise of will, I may indeed,
and do, at once reason that, when my neighbor
lifts a stone, he too must exercise his will in
order to exert the force; but I may not positively say that all manifestations of force, in
the earthquake, the tempest, the fire, must
likewise be the result of will-power. As far as
known to me will exists only under certain conditions and in certain relations, such as God
must be wholly independent of. But I may
say that God can and does exercise force such
as I can only exercise by an exertion of the
will, and that he can and does do infinitely
more and greater things than I can. What is
will-power in me, is power still in him, but
may be something infinitely greater, more
simple and perfect, than that limited form of it
which is exerted by the human will.

So also with intelligence and with the moral
attributes, which belong to the idea of personality. When another man, with like constitution and in like circumstances as mine, arranges

his deeds in such an order and combination as
to bring about a certain end intended, I say he
is an intelligent being.   I reason from myself,
and have a right to do so in such a case.   But
even though Evolution shows me more clearly
and beautifully than ever was known before
how all forces and objects and events in the
whole universe are adjusted and adapted to one
another in a sublime harmony, and bring forth
definite results, I have no right to say that
thereby God's intelligence is proved.   Intelligence is a term of limitation and imperfection.
It is altogether a human quality, determined
by human conditions, and bringing about results by human processes of reasoning, choice,
and volition.   In God there may be nothing
at all analogous to such mental processes.
There is probably no process at all; but simply
the divine Being immediately, spontaneously,
continuously manifesting itself in this wise,
without the need of any such means as are the
intellect and will in man.   All I may, therefore,
affirm is that God produces results similar to
those I can produce only by the laborious exercise of various faculties of mind, but which
he may bring to pass spontaneously and immediately.

I may indeed call certain combinations of
deeds intelligent and wise, others righteous and
good; and can then say that all God's actions
are wise and good.   But I cannot apply those

terms to himself, lest I thereby misconceive and
degrade his infinite and absolute being. That
which produces all that is produced is probably
far more than wisdom and goodness. As the
indivisible God, immediately acting, he com-
prehends all partial conceptions under him. In
the divine nature what are intelligence, will,
goodness, but one and the same, the God-spirit,
not thinking, designing, willing, feeling, acting, but simply being himself, manifesting himself according to the eternal order of his being?

" ' Yes, write it in the rock!' Saint Bernard said,
  ' Grave it on brass with adamantine pen!
   'Tis God himself becomes apparent, when
   God's wisdom and God's goodness are displayed.' " [20]

Just as the eternal immanence of God's self
is that which on the one hand is manifested as
gravitation, whose very existence constitutes
the law which governs all nature, so that same
divine immanence manifesting itself on the
other hand in the spiritual realm, may itself
constitute by its very presence, the laws of
intelligence and morality, of Truth, Beauty,
and Goodness, according to which all spirit is
governed. Who knows but we shall yet realize
Emerson's profound prophecy, and some day
"shall see the identity of the law of gravitation
with purity of heart; and . . . . that the
Ought, that Duty, is one thing with Science,

---

[20] Matthew Arnold—The Divinity.

with Beauty, and with Joy."[21] Aye, who would not rejoice if, when no longer seeing "through a glass darkly," but knowing even as also we are known, we should realize that goodness and wisdom, and all other such terms, are but names, like red, yellow, and blue, of a few reflected rays of the ineffable Light of the world, while the eternal Source thereof is himself different from each and infinitely more than the sum of them all?

This certainly would not detract from the divine personality. That which is alone essential to our being able to love God, to serve and obey him, and to address him as Thou, yea, even as Abba, our Father, is not that we conceive him as thinking, feeling, and willing, but that we know him as one being, and as absolutely free and self-determining spirit.

And these qualities no evolutionist can consistently deny. "Hear, O Israel, the Lord thy God is one God!" was no more positively and clearly revealed to the Hebrews through Moses, than it is reiterated to us through Evolution. As we have already seen, this whole philosophy is based on the discovery of the Persistence of Force; and the essential thing in that discovery is nothing less than the oneness of the Substance, the individual identity of that suprasensuous, non-material Being, of which all

---

[21] Address before Senior Class in Divinity College.

phenomena are but so many varied manifestations. Whether in condensing the nebula or
distilling the dew, whether in guiding the herds
of planets through space, or directing the
swarms of molecules in the air, it is one and
"the selfsame Spirit that worketh all in all."
There is one Power in the infinite variety of
manifestations. There is one God who rules
all and whom all must obey. Unity in the
midst of diversity; no conflict of plans or agencies; absolute harmony; universal co-operation.
This is what Evolution so positively declares
and reveals to us, and this is whereby it has
forever made pantheism impossible.

That this "one God and Father of us all" is
a self-determining Power follows necessarily
from the fact that he is absolute, almighty, and
omnipresent. He manifests himself not as
confusion, but as order. He produces good and
wise results. Some determination, if so we must
call it, is plainly implied in this. If it were a
determination imposed by another, God were
not absolute. Whatever determination there is
must therefore be God's own, perfectly free, entirely independent, from within, not from without. He is the only First Cause. He is himself
the determination of himself and of all things.

Only of such a Being can love be predicated.
Though here we must again take heed not to
be misled by this word into the baldest anthropomorphism. God's love cannot be the same

3

as our love. The term is only used as a partial, approximate designation. In man its chief characteristics are subjective. Of God's subjective condition we know nothing whatever. But when I love I so act as to produce beneficent results to the object of my love. Therefore, when I see beneficence all around, produced everywhere by the divine Power, I reason that this Power is likewise moved by love. As absolute, however, he cannot be moved at all. Of feelings, intentions, impulses in him we know nothing. All I can legitimately mean, therefore, is that God is a Being who produces beneficent results. And as it appears that in the largest sense all his effects are such, we must conclude that the divine nature is such as invariably to result in beneficence; beneficence is the expression of his essential being. In this sense then "God is love;" and Dr. Samuel Harris is certainly right when he declares that "Mr. Spencer demonstrates that the law of love is the ultimate ground of the law of nature and the reign of love its ultimate issue and end. He already knows the unknowable to be Power. Here he demonstrates that it is Love; and therefore God: for God is love." [22]

Beneficence is the order, principle, law of God's manifestation; but whether as a princi-

---

[22] Philosophical Basis of Theism.

ple it is at all akin to the sentiment of love as
known in man, we cannot know. All we do
know is that, unlike man's love, the love of
God abideth, is eternal and infinite, perfect
and absolute as himself; because it is himself.
And as all other ethical principles are in the
last place included under this and resolvable
into it, Right, Truth, Goodness, Beauty must
also be regarded as so many aspects of the order
of divine manifestation, and as such as real,
universal, and eternal principles of being immanent in the world with God, in God. Are
they not the divine Expression, Logos, Word
that was "in the beginning," that was with
God, that was God? This is their warrant.
This gives them their absolute and their sacred
character.

It will have become apparent ere now that
this conception of God is far different from the
one of popular theology. In place of a Creator
working at the world from the outside, it shows
us an inherent, all-pervasive Power, permeat-
ing all things, active everywhere, constantly
unfolding himself according to the eternal order
of his own being. Instead of an arbitrary
Lawgiver imposing his decrees upon the world,
or himself subject to moral laws existing somewhere or other in the universe, we have a spiritual Substance, whose own constitution and
mode of being are the eternal law of both
material and spiritual existence, determining

the "stream of tendency" that is ever "making for righteousness" and happiness, moulding all things great and small according to the principles of his own being. We have a God whom indeed we cannot picture as seated on a throne, invested with human form and attributes; but whom we can realize as being with us "alway even to the end of the world," as immediately present everywhere, as one in whom indeed and in truth we can "live and move and have our being;" a Spirit-principle who can actually live in us, whom we can "put on," on whom as a Foundation we can build up ourselves unto the ideal set before us. A God whom we can trust, because he is "the same yesterday, to-day and forevermore," "in whom is no variableness nor shadow of turning," the one true God blessed forevermore. Whom we can love because in all his manifestations not fickle and imperfect human sentiment can be seen, but a perpetual outflow of purest beneficence ever the same. Whom we can serve, because we know what service of him means and whither it tends. A God who in the truest sense is our Father, our Friend, and our Saviour. A God who is a God, and not a man.

III.

PROVIDENCE.

"Are not two sparrows sold for a farthing? and one of them shall not fall to the ground without your Father. But the very hairs of your head are all numbered."

(MATTH. 10: 29, 30.)

"And we know that all things work together for good to them that love God."

(ROM. 8: 28.)

"The things and events of the world do not exist or occur blindly or irrrelevantly, but all, from the beginning to the end of time, and throughout the farthest sweep of illimitable space, are connected together as the orderly manifestations of a divine Power, and . . this divine Power is something outside of ourselves, and upon it our own existence from moment to moment depends."

(JOHN FISKE—*Address at Farewell Dinner to H. Spencer.*)

" The law which moves to righteousness,
Which none at last can turn aside or stay;
The heart of it is love, the end of it
Is peace and consummation sweet. Obey!"

(EDWIN ARNOLD—*The Light of Asia.*)

"This is, in fact, the great miracle of Providence, that no miracles are needed to accomplish its purposes."

(JEREMY TAYLOR—*Natural History of Enthusiasm.*)

"The things that befall thee accept as well-wrought, knowing that without God nothing occurs."

(*The Teaching of the Twelve Apostles.*)

III.

PROVIDENCE.

THE old heathenish view of God as a vast man enthroned somewhere in space, and ruling, or rather playing with the earth from there, alone made possible the old theory of Providence.

According to this, the physical universe is governed by a set of "laws of nature," imposed upon it at the creation. But these laws are rather sovereign decrees than anything else. They are not inherent in the nature of things. They have no vital connection. They can be amended, annulled, suspended, and interfered with at the sweet will of the Lawgiver. And man is not subject to them at all in any real and definite sense; but directly and immediately dependent upon the good graces of an arbitrary Ruler, who to favor one will keep fire from burning, water from wetting, cold from freezing; will stay the action of gravitation, or break the eternal chain of causality; will do this at one place without its affecting the law in any other, and for one person without regard to all the rest of mankind and of the universe. Everything is governed, if not by chance, yet by whim. God has indeed a general plan and purpose, something like a chess player behind his board. But, like the latter, he changes the details, at least, of his plan to meet particular contingencies that constantly arise.

Not only is this view entirely at variance with the principles of true religion as revealed in the Bible; but it is harmful in every respect, as all untruth must be. It makes existence uncertain and precarious, subject to indefinite interference and interposition from without. It destroys true piety and faith in the life and conduct of men, tending to make them careless and derelict. And too often it is made but a presumptuous excuse for ignorance, laziness, and sinful neglect of duty; even as it encourages self-righteousness, vanity, and self-conceit, from which alone the doctrine can have sprung.

> " Scratched by a fall, with moans
> As children of a weak age
>   Lend life to the dumb stones
> Whereon to vent their rage,
> And bend their little fists and rate the senseless ground;
>   So, loath to suffer mute,
> We, peopling the void air,
>   Make Gods to whom to impute
> The ills we ought to bear;
> With God and Fate to rail at, suffering easily!" [1]

What is it, for instance, but self-conceit which animates the devout deacon,—who is also somewhat interested in certain railway stock—

---

[1] Matthew Arnold—Empedocles on Etna.

when he comes to me and exclaims, "Do you
know the A. B. C. road has gone up? Yes, sir,
and I had ten thousand and more invested in
it; but most providentially I got wind of how
matters were going, and succeeded in selling out
not more than an hour before the news became
generally known, and the stock was not worth
a cent any more!" That deacon plainly imagines himself a special favorite of Providence;
and that Providence actually helped him cheat
his neighbor! His faith will make him bolder
in his speculations and encourage him to cheat
again.

Not for a moment would I deny that there
was a Providence in the case. But there was
no interference or interposition. There was no
special favor shown the deacon by God, much
rather the contrary. There had been an opportunity given him to show forth true honesty
and integrity; he refused to take it; he made it
a means for strengthening himself in dishonesty;
and by so much it will hasten on the penalty
for breaking a moral law that will come upon
him. The evil lies in the deacon's wrong interpretation of the circumstance, that is, in his
altogether erroneous and immoral idea of Providence. He presumptuously attributed a purpose
to God for which there was no ground but his
own self-conceit and corrupt character. And
that is the great mistake and evil of the whole
popular conception of Providence, over and

above the wrong views of divine being and methods which it involves.

Equally irreligious and immoral is the false trust in Providence resultant, from such a view. The ignorant religionists who refuse to put up lightning-rods, and think it wrong to be vaccinated, are only consistent in their error. But they are not more pious than others. A minister of the gospel refused positively to have any medicine administered to his child which was sick. "It is in the hands of Providence," he said. And men were found to admire and commend his "simple and childlike trust!" "It is a visitation of Providence," solemnly exclaimed another, two members of whose family had already died of typhoid fever, while a third was even then suffering from diphtheria; "It is a visitation of Providence, and I humbly bow before his will!" But he did not repair the leak in his drain-pipe that had undermined his cellar and yard, and made it a morass of filth and poisonous corruption.

It is such cases as these, still only too plentiful, and too leniently regarded, that have set many men against the whole doctrine of Providence, of which they are nothing but a gross perversion. They recognize the untruth in such views, and that they work incalculable harm in the world. Particularly is Providence as thus represented combated and ridiculed by scientists, who see how it would destroy all coherence in the universe, and deny that sublime unity of nature which is more and more being revealed by the researches and discoveries that are being made in every sphere of existence, and which Evolution especially has demonstrated and illustrated to an extent little dreamed of as possible a few years ago.

More and more clearly is it being shown that any view which loses sight of the unity, continuity, and regular order manifested in the world, must be erroneous, and can only detract from the dignity and perfection of him of whose essential being these qualities are the beautiful expression. Thoughtful men recognize the truth expressed by Mr. Spencer, that "Irregularity of method is a mark of weakness. Uniformity of method is a mark of strength. Continual interposition to alter a prearranged set of actions, implies defective arrangement in those actions. The maintenance of those actions, and the working out by them of the highest results, implies completeness of arrangement. If human workmen, whose machines as at first constructed require perpetual adjustment, show their increasing skill by making their machines self-adjusting; then, those who figure to themselves the production of the world and its inhabitants by a 'Great Artificer,' must admit that the achievement of this end by a persistent process, adapted to all contingencies, implies greater skill than its achievement by the process of meeting the contingencies as they severally arise." [2]

It is plain that, to be believed by all, a doctrine must be worthy of belief. And in order to this, the doctrine of Providence must not involve any impious imputation of motives and purposes to God of which we can know nothing. It must not furnish any ground or excuse for self-righteousness, ignorance, and irreligion in man. Nor, finally, must it belittle the greatness and perfection of God. It must be true to known facts; consistent with itself; and helpful to man. No other doctrine is worthy of belief; no other will be accepted by the growing intelligence of the times; and none other finds any warrant in the principles of Christianity or of Evolution.

The true Christian doctrine which meets all these requirements fully is a necessary corollary from the conception of God we arrived at in the preceding Study; and as such, religion and Evolution are not only at one with reference to it, but the teachings of the latter explain and sustain those of the former to the fullest extent possible. Recognizing God, not as a Being outside of the world and ruling it from without in an arbitrary, lawless manner, but as a spiritual Power, immanent in the universe, and manifesting himself through "an ever-present

---

[2] Principles of Biology, vol. i.

and all-pervading divine energy," as Prof. Le Conte calls the forces of nature, according to a uniform method, "universal because he is omnipresent, invariable because he is unchangeable,"[*] we see Providence to be nothing but God unfolding himself; the expression in the world of his inherent nature; subordinating, subjecting all things and occurrences thereto; bringing all into conformity with himself. This view was hinted at by Prof. Fiske at the farewell banquet tendered to Mr. Spencer at New York on the eve of his leaving this country after his too brief visit, when he said: "The things and events of the world do not exist or occur blindly or irrelevantly, but all, from the beginning to the end of time, and throughout the furthest sweep of illimitable space, are connected together as the orderly manifestations of a divine power, and this divine power is something outside of ourselves, and upon it our own existence from moment to moment depends."

There is nothing unreliable, fickle, uncertain, about such a Providence; nothing irregular or incoherent in his methods; in him is "no variableness neither shadow of turning." The very same order by which the first night followed the first day, still persists, ever has persisted, and ever will; providentially so ordered that

---

[*] Princeton Review, November, 1878.

all earthly creatures may positively reckon on
it, and conform their lives and works accord-
ingly; never arbitrarily altered or suspended
even for a single hour, to suit the short-sighted
wishes of this one or that one who might have
refused to co-ordinate his little affairs with it;
but always wisely and beneficently maintained
for the comfort and undisturbed existence of
millions of worlds above, and myriads of lives
in the plant and insect and animal world below. The identical order according to which
bloom the twinkling "flowers of the sky," and
move the sun and moon and planets, and remains stable the foundation of earth, on which
all life depends, has been preserved from everlasting, nor consented to be changed because,
forsooth, some heedless creature might have
walked too near a precipice! The eternal order
by which he might be kept from falling was
providentially established, nor would be suspended a moment because he preferred to fly
in its face and be dashed to pieces. The same
laws were always operating, the same conditions always existing, by conforming to which
he might avoid the precipice, or falling, might
yet save himself from injury or death. It was
by the inexorable unchangeableness and certainty of Providence's operations that the one specu-
lator lost and the other saved his money, and
by heeding which both might have been kept
from sacrificing their characters.

Always, in the invariability and absolute uniformity of Providence lies its true beneficence and wisdom. And if any change in the divine Being and his manifestations were thinkable, it would have to be at the expense of that wisdom and beneficence. For, as is freely admitted by all leading theologians, as for example by Dr. Fisher of Yale, "all the forces of nature are so interlinked in a system, that any single occurrence involves the more immediate or the more remote participation of all." Every minutest circumstance, therefore, every most trivial event, is causally connected with every circumstance and event of the remotest past as of the most distant future. It is the product that has grown out of the labor of the centuries. It is a seed-germ in which lie enfolded essential parts of the happiness and very existence of future ages. It is a necessary step in the march of universal being. It is a note in the sublime harmony of the spheres. To change it would be to abort the past, to rob the future, to throw the all into hopeless discord. Upon the absolute permanence of the methods of Providence, therefore, upon the fact that providential government is essentially government by law, depend its helpfulness to man, and its general beneficence.

And this permanence is proved not only by the history of the material universe, but especially by that of the human race. Not only do we learn from geology that, ages before man appeared upon the earth, the work of developing inorganic matter from a state of comparative chaos to one of harmony and beauty went on regularly, according to precisely the same laws that yet are in force;—not only are we taught that organisms were differentiated, and perfected in their growth, in the same order now yet revealed to us: first the seed, then the blade, and then the full ear, each plant and each animal producing after its kind, living according to known laws that still regulate all life;—but by the new science of sociology we are now also assured that man in all his relations to his fellow men, his marrying, his building, his travelling, his politics, his religion, follows the same fixed and certain order as in the beginning regulated his conduct under like circumstances. While it has indeed always been taught as a religious tenet that

> " There's a divinity that shapes our ends,
>   Rough-hew them how we will,"

it was left for sociology not only to demonstrate the tenet to be a scientific fact, no longer to be questioned or doubted by any one, but also to show that in this as in everything else, the divinity proceeds according to a regular order, certain and invariable; and thus to make the fact utilizable and of practical moment to man. It is true, the laws of sociology are by no means clearly understood as yet. The science is too young for us to expect that already; and perhaps the field is too intricate and profound for us ever to expect it. Still the fact has been established that here as everywhere there is law, there is real divine Providence.

And more than this, while Christianity and Evolution both deny that any one can understand the motives and purposes of God, whose thoughts are higher than our thoughts as the heavens are higher than the earth, and while both ask, "Who can tell what is good for man in this life?" they are at one as to the fact that the order of providential government is altogether beneficent. Just as the Bible ever implies and expressly declares that "all things work together for good," so science ever illustrates and enforces the same truth as expressed by Mr. Spencer, that "Slowly, but surely, evolution brings about an increasing amount of happiness;" and that "Evolution can end only in the establishment of the greatest perfection and the most complete happiness." [4] The only difference is that the latter attempts in some measure to explain how Providence does it, by what means and what method.

Accepting with religion the evidence of ethnology and history, that the differentiation of man into families, tribes, nations, and races was

[4] First Principles.

the result of providential leading and was an essential factor in the improvement and elevation of the physical, intellectual, and moral condition of humanity, Evolution gives the additional information that Providence did this, not by any interference with the laws of nature, nor in a lawless manner, but according to the methods of natural selection, sexual selection, the struggle for existence, the survival of the fittest, variation, heredity, by means of tendencies, appetites, desires, and thoughts, inherent in the human constitution. It does not thereby in any wise deny the beneficence of the results. This cannot be denied, unless one would refuse to acknowledge that the present state of man is better than his primitive condition. Through all the wars and intrigues, the migrations of nations, the founding and the downfall of dynasties and states in the past, it recognizes the action of that divine Power whose all-pervading energy moved and directed each detail as the whole grand total of history; and while with Cowper

> " Resolving all events, with their effects
> And manifold results, into the will
> And arbitration wise of the Supreme," [5]

it agrees rather with the healthier Milton than with the more melancholy bard, in affirming that

---

[5] The Task.

" All is best,—though we often doubt
What the unsearchable dispose
    Of highest wisdom brings about,—
And ever best found in the close."[6]

If there is such unanimity between religion
and Evolution as to what is commonly called
"general Providence," why should there be
any conflict between them on the subject of
"special Providence?" For it is here that
oftenest they are said to be at variance. I
think, however, it is all owing to the unfortunate use of the term "special Providence,"
which stands for no reality, nor is meant to
express any real difference in Providence itself
or in its methods. At least no intelligent
Christian will so use it.

Really there is no such thing as a special
Providence. Or, if you please, there is no
general Providence, but only a special. Every
occurrence is under the guidance of that omnipresent Power "that worketh all in all." He
not only holds the seas in the hollow of his
hand, but not a sparrow falleth to the ground
without him, and the very hairs of our head
are all numbered. It is the same Power that
condensed the limitless expanses of star-dust
nebulæ into globes and systems of worlds, and
that distils the atmospheric moisture into dia-
mond dew-drops; the same Energy that guides

---

[6] Samson Agonistes.

the myriad suns and planets through the fields of ether, and that whirls the autumn leaves a sombre flock through the forest. Realize this, and all difficulties about general and special Providence will vanish into nothing.

And this Evolution helps us to realize most vividly. According to its fundamental principle, that of the persistence of force, the divine Power is immediately present in every single occurrence that takes place anywhere. Absolutely nothing happens without God, without his direct and immediate presence and activity. So far the Christian's faith in the continual and abiding nearness of God, and sense of absolute dependence upon him is fully borne out by Evolution, and demonstrated in a manner comprehensible to all. The assurance that "He doeth all things well" is not weakened, but substantiated by the conviction forced upon us by Evolution that "By its essential nature, the process must everywhere produce greater fitness to the conditions of existence." Upon this, too, we can base a childlike, trustful hope for our individual selves. For if we are sure that all things conduce to the greatest good of all, then whatever happens to us, however seemingly evil for the present, must also eventually be for our own benefit, in so far as we are a part of the whole, and the advantage of the whole reflects to the real advantage of its every part.

This trust is indeed a source of peace and humble resignation to the divine guidance. But it is not all the Christian may have. Nor would it be enough to be of practical aid in his work and conduct of life. We want to know how God's presence and power are conditioned;) what determines the form and direction of his manifestation; how we may derive help and benefit therefrom. Plainly, if he manifests himself quite arbitrarily, according to no known method and order, the reign of Providence is not much different to us, in our practical work and in ordering our characters and lives, than would be the reign of chance. What we need to know is, not only that in a general way its results will be for good, and that ultimately the whole universe will be benefited and bettered, but especially how you and I may be benefited, according to what principles, on what conditions, you and I will receive good from the divine influence. What we are most interested in and concerned about is the good of us as individuals, and that too, not only the ultimate, but the immediate, present good.

And to a certain extent at least it is our privilege and even our duty to know this; even as it is a necessary prerequisite to true religious faith and trust. From his mere conviction that all that God does is well done, the farmer has no right nor power to trust Providence that it will keep it from raining to-morrow and ruining his crops. But in order really to have this trust and be justified in it, he must know enough of the meteorological laws to be able to tell whether the conditions of rain are present or absent. It the latter, then he will be able to give a reason for the hope that is in him; not otherwise. For without this knowledge his professed trust would either be mere hypocrisy, or the ignorant presumption that God, for this man's private convenience, would alter his eternally fixed order of procedure, and disregard the highest good of all the rest of the universe.

I am aware that by far the greater part of all the much-talked-of trust in Providence is nothing but just such hypocrisy or presumptuous ignorance. It is even thought by not a few that knowledge is incompatible with trustfulness. There is, however, no ground whatever, it is needless to say, for such an irreligious notion either in the Bible or in experience. All trust that is not based on knowledge, and willing to be conformed to it, is disappointed as often as not; and is never capable of influencing for good the life of him who holds it.

I know that the theory of Providence now taught in our orthodox systems of theology differs, seemingly, but only seemingly, from the popularly held ones that we have considered. According to it God has so ordered every minutest detail of occurrence in the world as to

accord with his preconceived purpose and plan.
When you stumble and fall, for example, it is
indeed the immediate result of your not seeing
the stone in your path, and this is the result of
your attention having been attracted to a kick-
ing horse on the street, and this again has a
complication of other causes, and so on along
the chain of causality, until it becomes too
intricate to follow, back to the will of God who
ordained that all these causes and events should
so work together as to bring about, just at that
moment of time, just that particular occurrence, to wit: your stumbling over that stone;
and all this, *in order that* you should fall.

The objections to this view are the same as
those against the popular one, as, indeed, the
latter is really the same as the former, only in
a cruder form. It ascribes intentions and purposes to the divine Being for which there is no
warrant anywhere. It presumes to know the
inscrutable mysteries of God's inmost being,
and comprehend his ways which are past finding out. It degrades the conception of the
divine by making it essentially like the human
nature. And none the less than the popular
view, it either supposes a change in, or at least
an addition to, the original forms of God's
manifestation; or it necessitates an ultra-Cal-
vinistic fatalism. Either every minutest detail
has been pre ordained and fixed from all eternity, or some where in the past, in that vague

complication of causes where the mind can no
longer follow the separate threads, there was a
new direction given, in order to which new
causes and conditions must have been created,
with a view to the future stumbling and falling.

The view which alone Evolution warrants,
and which I before tried to explain, lays itself
open to none of these objections. It presumes
to no knowledge of God's preconceived intentions. The events and occurrences of the world
it simply accepts as the results of the continuous
unfolding of the divine Being, the uniformity
and regularity of which constitute the order or
laws of nature. Nor is there ever any change
or modification made in this order. From all
eternity it is fixed that whoever does not look
to his footsteps and encounters a stone in his
path, will stumble and fall over that stone.
Had the man in our illustration had faith enough
in Providence to conform himself to this divine
order, he would not have fallen. As it was, he
disregarded Providence, and incurred the natural penalty, he fell. It was according to
providential method, by providential means.
Providence was in it from beginning to end.
But a Providence recognizable by science, intelligible to reason, and not contrary to Scripture.

The Bible expressly tells us that "all things
work together for good *to them that love God.*"
The promise of safety and special protection is
never promiscuously made; but ever only to

them who are true servants and followers of
God. They are the only ones not a hair of
whose heads shall be touched for harm. And
this theology shows us to mean, and Evolution
confirms it as the only possible meaning, that
only those whose whole purpose is bent on
making their lives conform with the life of God
as far as known, whose spirits are subject to
his Spirit, have any reason or right to trust in
his Providence. For only this is true love and
service of God: to recognize the beneficence of
the divine order everywhere, to become more
fully acquainted with it, and to care more for
its fulfillment and unhindered action, than for
our own little selfish wishes, intentions, and
projects. In direct proportion to the degree of
such love in any one's heart, is that one's union
with God; the more fully one has thus renewed
his mind, and presented himself, body, soul,
and spirit a living sacrifice to him, the more
fully will he "prove what is that good, and
acceptable, and perfect, will of God." Such
an one will have cause to expect with confidence to be cared for, protected, guided, and
blessed by the divine Providence; not through
any interposition of the latter, any interference
with the regular course of divine manifestation,
but through his own subjection to and conformity with this very order; not through any
alteration or suspension of God's laws, but
through his own obedience to these laws,

through his own becoming an integral part and
co-agent in the eternal harmony of the universe.
And even those occurrences which others would
call adverse and unfortunate, he will at once
gladly and freely recognize and accept as boons
and blessings, corrections which shall tend
better to instruct him, means to assist him in
the future fuller and more complete adaptation
and adjustment of himself to the divine. Such
occurrences will often happen in the present
imperfect knowledge of God and his laws. But
they will never be really contrary to the true
Christian servant's will; for he has no positive
will except where he knows it to be in accord
with God's being and methods.

How different the trust of such an one is from
that pseudo-trust which too many profess, and
with which they bring the whole blessed doctrine of Providence into disrepute and scorn!
And how materially Evolution helps him in it!

First of all, humility enters into all true trust,
as into all true religion. And he who has it
does not get up in prayer-meeting and say, "I
was going to town on the very train that was
wrecked this morning; but providentially our
carriage-wheel came off, and we were detained
until after the train had started. I feel that
indeed the Lord takes care of his own!" and
then sit down with a look at the poor publicans
around that plainly says, "I thank Thee, Lord,
that I am not like other men; or even like

these!" But, while gratefully confessing that even the coming off of his carriage-wheel was providential, he does not think nor imply that it was because of his superior piety, or because he was a special favorite of God. He is not elated, but more deeply bowed down. For he knows that the same Providence that was in his detention was also in the wreck from which hundreds of his fellow men, as good and pious as himself, were made to suffer. And that, in both, the divine agency was according to fixed laws and conditions; not on that account, however, less providential; nor more so than the day before when the train was not wrecked and he not detained. Though the result would have been, perhaps, less painful, if, the providentially fixed conditions of a safe journey being known, they had been more carefully complied with.

It is a lack of humility that sees Providence in that which conduces to its own convenience more than in anything else; that imagines the indulgence of its own wishes and whims of more importance and significance than the regular process of divine beneficence that is going on every moment in every nook and corner of the whole universe; or that presumes to believe that all the eternal chain of past and future events was designed and adjusted so as to meet its insignificant approbation; instead of seeing and gratefully appreciating the far more sublime and blessed fact that it, in spite of its littleness and unworthiness, may and must adjust and adapt itself to this eternal order and become a living, co-operating part of the same.

Humility realizing this, dutifulness then makes all true trust a living, active, working trust, and him who holds it a "laborer together with God." Knowing how many of his ways are incomprehensible and unsearchable, the real believer will not blame Providence for any disappointment or misfortune, but will attribute it always to his own ignorance or neglect. If he falls down the stairs in the dark, he will neither complain of the "mysterious visitation of Providence," nor afterward lie down and simply "trust to Providence" to set his broken leg. But he will confess that the means of lighting his lamp and descending the stairs in safety had been providentially given him, but been neglected by him. And he will accept the fall as a providential assistance to him not to fall the next time. Moreover he will quickly send for the best physician, so firmly trusting Providence as to consider it a duty to use every means known through which Providence might heal the fractured bone, and restore to health his shattered frame.

So always. The only trust for which there is any warrant in the Scriptures, and which is in full agreement with Evolution also, accepts the established order of divine manifestation, and seeks in every way possible to become more fully acquainted, and to bring itself into accord and harmony, with it. It does not go into the house of a small-pox patient, or eat unwholesome food, or expose itself to wet and cold and malarial damps, and then trust Providence to preserve it in health and strength. Nor does it store nitro-glycerine in the cellar, or pour kerosene oil into the stove, or give the children matches to play with, and then place its trust in Providence to guard it against calamity by fire. This would be no trust at all, but mockery. Real, worthy Christian trust learns what it can of the laws of health, and conforms its conduct to them. It removes all the conditions and possible causes of fire. And then it has a reason for its confidence, and will not be disappointed therein. Where it is disappointed, it will find by investigation that it was not through the failure of any of the providential laws, but invariably through some failure of its own, through ignorance or carelessness, to adapt itself fully to these laws.

In a word, the trust of love, the only Christian trust, accepts God's ways of working instead of man's, and adopts the former in place of the latter, as far as it is able. And thus "the Spirit allies himself with every faculty of ours to quicken and to strengthen it, and to work through it for good," in the words of Canon Fremantle of Canterbury; thus is "the Divine order established in our renewed nature, the surest witness that we are made in the image of God, the spiritual mind by which we see each part of the universe in its relation to its center, and evolving itself under the Divine purpose towards complete organization and perfect harmony." [1]

I am well aware that many will object to this view as taking away from the conception of Providence that element of uncertainty, mystery, unreliability, which to them is essential, and substituting the reign of law. But is not the Duke of Argyll correct when he says, "Creation by Law—Evolution by Law—Development by Law, or, as including all these kindred ideas, the Reign of Law, is nothing but the reign of Creative Force directed by Creative Knowledge, worked under the control of Creative Power and in fulfillment of Creative Purpose"? [2] As the laureate puts it,

" God is law, say the wise; O Soul, and let us rejoice,
For if He thunder by law the thunder is yet His voice." [3]

And I am convinced that our view is in no particular gainsaid by any of the principles of the Christian religion, while it is the only view compatible with the principles of Evolution and the revelations of scientific observation.

---

[1] The Gospel of the Secular Life.
[2] The Reign of Law.
[3] The Higher Pantheism.

The Bible and Evolution, then, are at one with regard to what is called general Providence, that all things are guided and controlled by a Supreme Power, according to fixed laws, and are made to tend to the greatest good of all. As to special Providence the Bible just as clearly and positively declares that it is conditioned; and in a general way, it tells us what these conditions are: love to God. What is this but saying that Providence acts strictly according to law? Now all that Evolution does is more fully to explain and interpret this, to tell us in what this love to God must consist, and how it must act. This explanation may, indeed, contradict the old notion that the love of God, religion, is nothing but a mental state having no relation to or influence on our lives; but it certainly does not contradict the teachings of the Bible in any sense.

Nor does our view deprive the Christian of any of the comforting and sustaining power of his childlike confidence and trust in the overruling presence of him whose leading is altogether good and beneficent. As I tried to show, it rather strengthens it, by making his presence more vividly realizable, and enforces it by its full illustration and proof of the beneficence of his ways. It does, moreover, warn the truly devout against misplacing their trust, and show them where and how they ought to place it in order to avoid the danger of making a mistake and being disappointed; not upon their own merit or righteousness, nor upon any supposed human feelings, motives, impulses, in God; but only and directly upon God himself as he manifests his being and mode of action in the beneficent order of the universe everywhere. Wherever they do not fully understand this divine order and its conditions, as in the great majority of instances must as yet be the case, they are told that to expect it to be such as always suits their individual pleasure or convenience, is not trust, but presumption, and are pointed to the facts of experience in evidence that they will be disappointed oftener than not. Genuine trust in such cases will go no further than with firm confidence to expect that the greatest good of all will be promoted, and will accept with humble resignation whatever particular lot may fall to itself, knowing that itself is a means and condition in the furtherance of the destiny of the whole.

And, finally, knowing this, the earnest believer will ever make it the highest aim of his life to know more and more of God and his ways, and to work actively in accord with them; not sitting idly by and waiting for Providence "his wonders to perform," but realizing that God manifests himself in and through him as well as everywhere else, he will diligently labor in the department in which he finds himself, not for the indulgence of his own whims and fancies, but along the line pointed out to him in the whole course of animate and inanimate nature, for the consummation of that divine perfection for which the ages have been striving, to which the fingers of the past are pointing and the angels of the future beckoning, rejoicing that even he is chosen to work hand in hand with the whirling of the planets, the shining of the myriad suns, the lightnings of heaven and the heaving of the earth, with saints and sages, heat and light and gravitation, with all the elemental powers and vast cosmic forces; his heart throbbing with God's own heart, his life helping to swell the harmony of God's eternal being,

> " That God which ever lives and loves,
> One God, one law, one element,
> And one far-off divine event,
> To which the whole creation moves." [10]

---

[10] Tennyson—In Memoriam.

IV.

PRAYER.

"Verily, verily, I say unto you, Whatsoever ye shall ask the Father in my name, he will give it you."

(JOHN 16: 23.)

"The effectual fervent prayer of a righteous man availeth much."

(JAMES 5: 16.)

"It is said that evolution destroys prayer. Well, for those who use prayer as beggary, it does, it ought to. It is only natural that men should cry under stress for special things: but prayer, real prayer, is communion."

(HENRY WARD BEECHER—*Evolution and Revolution.*)

"Faith, dependence, love, obedience, self-surrender, and the unity and activity of will,—these constitute the laws and spirit of prayer."

(P. C. MOZOOMDAR—*The Oriental Christ.*)

"In prayer the intelligent believer does not invoke a different Power from that which is manifested in all the forms of physical energy which are manifested in nature; he does but invoke the *same* Power, and the *only* Power which is the source of all causation, and produces all the processions of phenomena."

(B. F. COCKER—*Theistic Conception of the World.*)

"When there is a way by which God can answer prayer without disturbing his own laws, it is safest to conclude that this is the actual method employed."

(JAMES McCOSH—*Method of Divine Government.*)

IV.

PRAYER.

THE doctrine of prayer is intimately and vitally connected with that of Providence. According to the view we take of the latter will be our view of the former. If, therefore, the conclusions of our preceding Study were correct, we should have no great difficulty in arriving at a satisfactory view of prayer, satisfactory to the Christian Bible student and the Christian evolutionist alike.

As we had to reject the old but still popular idea of Providence, that regards God as adapting himself and the outer world to man, and substitute for it the truer one that God gives man the knowledge and means to adjust himself to the divine being and order; so will we find the conception of prayer, as to its essential nature, its mode of expression, and its end, which alone is substantiated by observed facts, alone is in accord with the principles, or at least the general spirit and trend, of Evolution, and alone is fully sanctioned by the principles and reconcilable with the teachings of Scripture, to be different from the old but still theoretically current notions on the subject, and far more consistent with the whole spirit of Christianity, worthier of responsible, rational beings, and more practically helpful, elevating, and inspiring in its influence upon man.

Prayer is universal. We know man only as a praying creature. From the earliest ages he has prayed. And Milton aptly describes, as characteristic of the first human pair, how at the close of the first day,

> " at their shady lodge arrived, both stood,
> Both turned, and under open sky adored
> The God that made both sky, air, earth, and heaven,
> Which they beheld; the moon's resplendent globe,
> And starry pole:" [1]

The lowest aboriginal Australian after his fashion prays to his fetich. The native African, in his bamboo hut, prays to his Shaman, and his Shaman in fantastic rite bears his prayers to his deity. The fierce Viking of the north, cowering on the deck of his boat, prayed to Thor whose thunders shake the sky, to Loki whose lightning rends the heavens. The Parsee bows before the sun; the Hebrew bends before Jehovah; the Greek and Roman, Hindu and Aztec, Pagan and Christian, man everywhere and always has prayed, and ever and in all places will pray. It may be to false gods or to true, it may be from superstition or religion, from fear or from love, yet the fact of prayer remains, and with it the fact of a fundamental

---

[1] Paraside Lost.

instinct or impulse prompting to it, deep down in the roots of human nature, always the same whatever new elements may be ingrafted upon it, into whatever variety of form it may flower and whatever fruit it may bear.

And like every wild stock of nature in which there is inherent good, it has shown itself capable of culture and improvement. It has obeyed the law of development with wonderful pliability, adapted itself to vast changes in its environment, and ever survived in higher, purer, and better forms, until to-day we scarce would be willing to recognize as real those earlier and crude feelings and expressions which once took the place of what now is alone acknowledged to be prayer, were it not that the original stock still flourishes to so remarkable an extent, and that reversals to the earliest forms are still common. For practically, among the masses of intelligent Christians even, the conception and practice of prayer are but little advanced beyond those not only of a thousand years ago, but of the age of Shamanism and Fetich-worship.

It is this very fact that repels so many of the more thoughtful to the extreme of not believing in nor practicing prayer at all. They know only of the crude conception, and even perhaps without being able to give a definite reason against it, yet feel that it is out of accord with man's present knowledge and views, not adjustable to the present state of moral and intel-

lectual culture. The wild plant is out of place
in, out of harmony with, the rest of the spiritual garden of to-day. So that while all professed Christians at least still observe the forms
of prayer, there lurks in the hearts of too many
a strong disbelief in its use and efficacy. The
blame is not theirs so much as of those who
have neglected and refused to cultivate and
improve the doctrine of prayer up to the general
standard required, to rid it of what is erroneous
or unessential, to refine its dross away, and to
adapt its essential truth to the other truths of
religion; in other words, to bring it into equilibrium with the rest of the spiritual world.

I would not, however, be understood as saying that no improvement at all has been made
in the past in this matter. The doctrine of
prayer as to-day held and explained by theologians is vastly in advance of the doctrine
taught even only a century ago. Indeed there
is probably no other subject in theology which
has undergone more evident and even radical
changes, and oftener, to adapt it to the growth
of human intelligence than just this one. I
cannot but feel, however, that the modifications
therein have not kept pace with the enlargement of our ideas of the divine being and government that have been brought about chiefly
by the immense progress made in the natural
sciences within the last few decades, and the
co-ordination of their facts and discoveries under

the general principles of Evolution. In all the current schemes of theology so much at least of the old popular notions is still retained as limits the form of expression to thought and speech, and makes its purpose and end the conformity of God to man. In so far there is little or no advance made by theology from the view held by the general Christian public. The only difference is that the latter asks and expects God to suspend, or break in upon, the uniform order of his manifestation by direct and immediate interposition; while the former supposes, according to Dr. Fisher, that "in answering prayer, God may interpose, not *manifestly* as in the case of a miracle, but, by the control which He exercises over the laws of Nature, may modify the effect of their action."—"The modification of causes may take place back of all proximate forces, in a region which science cannot penetrate. . . The intervention of Deity is out of sight, among the remoter forces that are nearer the primitive fountain of power in Himself."[2] Both expect by prayer to bring about some kind of "interposition," some "intervention of Deity;" whether "manifestly" or "out of sight" is unessential.

This view is very properly rejected by Dr. McCosh, a theologian fully alive to the requirements of reason and science, who thinks it is

---

[2] The Grounds of Theistic and Christian Belief.

not "needful to suppose that God interposes to change his own laws. The analogy of his method of operation in other matters would rather incline us to believe that he has so arranged these laws, that by their agency he may answer prayer without at all interfering with them." Therefore his theory is thus expressed: "When the question is asked, How does God answer prayer? we give the . . . reply—it is by a preordained appointment, when God settled the constitution of the world, and set all its parts in order."[3] But, alas, this in turn is not satisfactory to Dr. Fisher, who very truly says that, "It is felt by many to be an objection to this view that if nothing is to occur except what causes already in operation virtually contain, it seems like praying about what is past and beyond recall."[4]

Aside from its significance as showing the general dissatisfaction with the current theories of prayer, this difference between two of the most learned and representative theologians of the present day, shows the difficulty, the im-

---

[3] Method of Divine Government. Cf also the following, from "Realistic Philosophy," vol. i.—

"From the very beginning the prayer and its answer have been bound together in the counsels of heaven and the decrees of God. To accomplish his ends and to answer prayer it is not necessary that God should change his laws, for his unchanging laws may bring what is prayed for."

[4] Grounds of Theistic and Christian Belief.

possibility, of maintaining any view that requires as its basis a belief in a God outside of
and above the universe, governing it from
without by a set of arbitrary decrees, to be
modified, changed, interfered with at his pleasure, or at the request of any of his creatures;
and that regards man as separate and distinct
from the rest of nature, for whose benefit and
use alone nature exists. It is safe to say that
no doctrine of prayer will be acceptable to men
whose faith is governed by their knowledge,
and must harmonize with the prevalent modes
of thought, which is built upon such a foundation. For it is one entirely unsupported by facts,
out of all accord with the principles which are
dominant in the world of thought, and having
no sufficient warrant in the sacred Scriptures.

I fully agree with Dr. Fisher that in this
matter "The materials for induction are complex, and scattered over a vast area. Besides
they are not of a nature to be tested in the
crucible, or weighed in the balance." Still,
I cannot fail to see, as every honest and un-
biased person, it appears to me, must see, that
there is not a single well-attested fact extant to
show that there has ever been the slightest
modification made in the regular order of divine
manifestation in the world in consequence of
mere requests preferred by men. There have

---

* Grounds of Theistic and Christian Belief.

been cases where persons have offered up petitions which have been followed by their fulfillment; where men have asked for rain, and rain
came; for safety in danger, and they were
preserved; for recovery from disease, and they
were cured; for a change of heart, and they
were converted. But not only is there no evidence whatever that these very same events
would not have occurred even if the petitions
had not been made; but there are vastly more
cases where the same requests were made, and
were not followed by their fulfillment. So
greatly does the latter class of facts outnumber
the former, that, in any other department of
observation, no one would hesitate a moment to
say that they proved conclusively that there
was no real connection between request and
fulfillment. In this case, I freely grant, such a
conclusion would be unwarranted. But I also
maintain that there is just as little in the facts
to prove that there exists such a connection as
is claimed. If the facts do not disprove anything, neither do they prove anything. It
is far better frankly to acknowledge this, than
to appeal to facts which can have no weight,
to the ordinary mind at least, so long as there
is such a multitude of equally well attested facts
to counterbalance them. Such appeals in the
pulpit do nothing but harm, even if not dealing,
as is still too often done, with instances of
"miraculous healing" and boasted and well-

advertised "faith-cures," such as periodically are reported from rural districts.

To make men believe in prayer, teach them a doctrine of prayer that does not contradict their experience, and does no violence to their other beliefs, and to the whole tenor and mode of their thought; a doctrine that does not raise and then leave unanswered the question, so deeply felt even by the gifted Hindu who lately visited our shores, and so earnestly tried to be answered by him, "How can man's supplications change the purposes of the Immutable? How can divine fore-knowledge be influenced by the petitions of little-sighted humanity?" * It cannot! says Evolution. It need not; it does not! declares the Bible.

It were needless to adduce any evidence that the principles of Evolution sanction no such view of prayer as that currently held. That is self-evident. No one has ever claimed that they do, nor, so far as I am aware, even dreamed of the possibility of such a thing. And no less certain, even if less evident, is it that there can be no sufficient support found for it in the Scriptures. On the contrary, all the statements there made by Christ and his Apostles with reference to prayer, are so conditioned and qualified as to make the popular theory utterly irreconcilable with them; even while they point

---

* P. C. Mozoomdar—The Oriental Christ.

so clearly to the true view that one marvels how any other can ever have gained currency among believers.

Everywhere the promises of answer to prayer are made only to them that believe. Faith is the condition *sine qua non.* And faith is never a mere mental act, nor capable of being expressed in words alone. "Faith without *works* is dead, being alone." Ever the prayer that availeth must be "the *effectual* fervent prayer of a *righteous* man." Ever the assurance of being heard and answered is made by Christ only to them who "ask in my name," which, we are assured by the Hindu already quoted, who certainly is worthy of being heard, as entering more deeply into the full meaning of oriental phraseology than we colder occidentals can, "carries with it the hidden and profound significance of character. Unless therefore one is purified by shedding sympathetic blood over the emblem of Calvary, and risen with the resurrection of the Son of Man, how dare he ask anything in the name of Christ? Will crying, 'Lord, Lord,' avail on that day when the commandments about self-denial, crucifixion of the flesh, faith, love to man, asceticism, and seeking first the kingdom of God, are set at defiance?"' In other words, to pray in the name of Christ is more than to make a request.

' P. C. Mozoomdar—The Oriental Christ.

And finally, the Bible view is directly opposed to the notion that the purpose or end of prayer should be the conformity of God and his ways to man. The essential spirit of all true prayer is expressly declared to be "not my will, but thine, O God, be done!" This was the burden of Christ's petition when in his bitter agony he asked the Father to remove the cup from him. And the cup was not removed. The Father would not conform to the Son's expression of feeling; but, instead, the Son conformed himself to the Father, and thereby the deeper, permanent spirit of his prayer was answered. So Paul asked thrice that the thorn in his flesh might be taken away. But it was not taken. Instead of the divine being conformed to the human, the latter was made to adapt itself to the divine, and thus the inner spirit of the Apostle's true prayer was satisfied. And so ever, that prayer alone avails which, in the words of our deep-seeing Quaker poet,

> " brings to God's all-perfect will
> That trust of his undoubting child,
> Whereby all seeming good and ill
> Are reconciled.

> And, seeking not for special signs
> Of favor, is content to fall
> Within the providence which shines
> And rains on all." [8]

---

[8] The Hermit of the Thebaid.

The experience of Jesus and of Paul has been the experience of millions before and since their time. And so far a million facts, which may neither prove nor disprove anything with regard to the unsatisfying doctrine of prayer commonly held, furnish direct and positive evidence in favor of the view which, I think, is the only one that will harmonize with the principles of Evolution and of Scriptural religion alike. It is that the prayer of faith is expressed in deeds as well as words, and has for its purpose and end that God's will be done, that is, the conformity of man and of all things to the divine order of manifestation as far as known.

Facts show us that such prayer is fulfilled. The devout farmer who, in firm reliance on the beneficence of the divinely furnished means, prays for his daily bread by plowing the earth, sowing his seed, cultivating his field, and then in due season reaping his grain and taking it to the mill, will not be disappointed, but will surely receive an abundant answer to his prayer. God will assuredly give the increase, will make the seed spring up, will send the rain and the sunshine, will cause the field to bear rich fruit an hundredfold. The business-man who prays for success in his undertaking by using, in the spirit of confident faith, the God-given means of success, being prudent, diligent, persevering, and upright, will have his prayer answered every time. The mother who with yearning heart, with faith in the moral, mental and physical means supplied by God, and lovingly, wisely, untiringly using these means, prays that her children may be preserved from sin and brought up in the nurture and admonition of the Lord, will rarely have cause to complain with broken heart and tearful eyes that a mother's prayers are so seldom heard. Pray for health with faith enough in God's laws of health to study and obey them, and sickness will be a stranger to you. Pray that your crops be not spoiled by the rain, by conforming your sowing and your harvest to the divinely ordained order of nature, and taking heed unto the clouds and winds. Pray for peace, by following after the things that make for peace; for faith and hope and love, by using all the various means afforded you whereby these graces are made to thrive in the heart. This is the kind of prayer that is heard daily in thousands of cases. It is the only view of prayer that has fact and experience to sustain it.

Nor do the facts prove too much, as some might be apt to suggest. While there are many who get their daily bread and more, who are successful in business, who have good crops, and yet who are notoriously unrighteous, this does not prove that the prayer of the righteous does not avail anything; but only that even the unrighteous are under the necessity of praying, and that they acknowledge it. They obey the physical conditions of prayer, and therefore reap the physical results in so far at least. But nothing more. They can get not a single moral blessing, no spiritual blessing, unless they first conform to the moral, spiritual law. And, further, in so far as the moral and physical are mutually dependent, the unrighteous man's prayer will be fruitless. As, for instance, in order to be permanently prosperous in business, the moral laws of honesty, industry, temperance and others, must also be conformed with; or, in order to enjoy immunity from disease, the spiritual laws of moderation, purity and the rest, must be complied with as well as the physical laws of health.

If we would deny the name of prayer to the physical element in it, on the ground that the just and the unjust alike practice it, then must we restrict prayer entirely to the realm of moral and spiritual forces and phenomena. This is attempted to be done by many. But it involves them in a great maze of difficulties; and is, moreover, needless, unwarranted by Scripture, and at variance with our conception of the grand unity of the all, which recognizes no fundamental and essential difference between physical and spiritual forces. All force is one. All phenomena are the manifestations of the one, same God. This Evolution has anew demonstrated, and it must enter into every theory that would receive its sanction and would be consistent with a more and more universally recognized truth.

Not less essential to its acceptance by those whose thought is influenced by the principles of Evolution, is the fact that the end of all true prayer must be the conformity of man with the divine, and not the opposite, as is supposed by the view still theoretically held by most persons. For this does not conflict, but is in full and direct accord, with that important part of the theory of Evolution which regards all life as but "the continuous adjustment of internal relations to external relations." True prayer, recognizing the uniform order subsisting in the universe as the expression of the divine being, and conscious of its own short-sightedness and ignorance over against the known beneficence of the divine order, would not set its own little plans and wishes in opposition to it, would not have it changed in any detail even for its own seeming comfort or convenience; but rather most earnestly desires and strives to adapt and adjust its own wants, feelings, and constitution to this order. It therefore consciously fulfills in the highest degree the conditions of life.

Then, too, this view entirely does away with the idea of any "interposition" or "interference" with the regular course of events and action or combination of forces, such as we know never happens. By making prayer itself a motive force and efficient cause, it accounts for the

facts observed and implied in all true answer to
prayer without calling in the aid of any merely
supposititious cause or agency, or purely hypothetical mode of divine manifestation; and puts
prayer into line with the other forces at work in
the world, as a link in the regular chain of causation, instead of a disturbing factor. As such
Evolution cannot deny it a place in the world-
scheme as an important factor in the development of mankind.

As itself the chief agency and means through
which God fulfills prayer, a view which had the
support of so devout and learned a theologian as
Schleiermacher, among others, its existence and
influence on earth from the earliest times must
be accepted as a scientific fact, without which it
is impossible adequately to account for some of
the most important psychological, sociological,
and religious phenomena. Leave Martin Luther's prayers out of consideration, and what
have you left of the indomitable Reformer?
Praying he nailed Rome's condemnation to the
church-doors of Wittenberg; praying he sang
faith and fire into Europe's heart; praying he
gave Germany her Bible; praying he struck the
shackles from the mind and conscience of the
world. The victory of Dunbar cannot be explained simply by the mighty fighting of Crom-
well and his Ironsides. For the mightiness of
this fighting itself needs to be accounted for;
and can be only as the continuation and consum-

mation of their mighty praying. The victory was
in answer to their prayers. Not by any intervention from above; but by means of the prayers
themselves, which filled them with such invincible courage, all-vanquishing pertinacity, and
made them use the means required to bring victory to their arms. The Pilgrims prayed for a
free country, and America is the answer to their
prayers. They did not only request it, however,
but they made it. Their prayers were put into
their deeds and into those of their successors.
They prayed by their lives; by their marvellous
fortitude and endurance in suffering and hard-
ships; their diligent tilling of an ungrateful soil,

> "breaking the glebe, and mowing the grass in the
> meadows,
> Searching the sea for its fish, and hunting the deer in the
> forest;"

their building school-houses and churches, high-
ways and cities;—their prayers were the force
that made them use every means and gift vouchsafed them by God for laying deep the foundations of a commonwealth of free men and women.
Can Evolution deny the existence and efficacy
of such prayer? And will the Christian refuse
to acknowledge its validity and the reality of
its wondrous results?

That prayer should be an activity of the whole
person is simply in accord, moreover, with the
known laws of psychology. Its motor-power
lies in what Sir William Hamilton would have

called the Conative Faculties, which "have reference only to the future, for conation is a longing,—a striving, either to maintain the continuance of the present state, or to exchange it for another;" "there is a want, and a tendency supposed, which results in an endeavor either to obtain the object, when the cognitive faculties represent it as fitted to afford the fruition of the want; or to ward off the object, if these faculties represent it as calculated to frustrate the tendency, of its accomplishment." [*] As such it involves not only the whole mind, but, and as a necessary consequence of this, also the action of the bodily faculties in obedience to the feelings and will. No strong desire and appetency can thoroughly vent and express itself in words alone. The arch words of Priscilla the Puritan maiden were the words of a philosopher,

"When one is truly in love, one not only says it, but shows it."

And all longing is alike in this, that it is never satisfied with merely telling its passion. It must do something besides. It uses every means available for its fulfillment, impelling the will to move the body to action. And the deeper and more intense the appetency, the more it requires every faculty, nerve, muscle, with which to vent itself. Prayer, therefore, as the expression of the deepest and most intense of all longings, cannot sit

---

[*] Lectures: Metaphysics.

still and merely talk. Its yearning must affect the will, and this must result in action; for as Mr. Spencer says, "the passing of volition into action is simply a completion of the discharge." [10] Of course, where the ability to act is wanting, or where the cognitive faculties forbid it as not practicable, the action may not be carried out. Still the fact remains that volition and endeavor are essentially a part of true prayer; and therefore that prayer is itself a chief means of its own fulfillment; a conclusion which, as we have already seen, is fully borne out by the facts in the case.

But while the essential spirit of all real prayer must ever be fundamentally the same, in so far as it depends upon and is regulated by the cognitive faculties, by reason and experience, its direction and mode of expression will change as knowledge grows and widens its sphere. The low savage prays to his fetich in a manner corresponding to his ignorance of the divine Being and order of manifestation. His prayers are bribes, promises, threats. He brings his offerings, or beats his fetich. His prayers are accompanied by exhausting physical exercises. But defective knowledge keeps him from exerting himself in anything like the right direction. Thus the New Zealanders regarded sickness, according to Yate, quoted by Lubbock, as "brought

---

[10] First Principles.

on by the Atua, who, when he is angry, comes to them in the form of a lizard, enters their inside, and preys upon their vitals till they die. Hence they use incantations over the sick, with the expectation of either propitiating the angry deity or of driving him away; for the latter of which purposes they make use of the most threatening and outrageous language." [11] The ancient Hebrew has not only a loftier conception of God, and therefore indulges in no more threats and abuse, though he still brings offerings and sacrifices and makes his vows, but he also has learned that God answers prayer through what are called natural means. So he adds to his petitions the anointing of the patient with oil, makes it part of the expression of his prayer. The still more enlightened Christian, who has a yet more true conception of God, and has learned more of the laws of health and cure, of not only the means by which prayer is answered, but also the order of answering, leaves his vows and offerings away entirely, and vents his prayer in applying the remedies, doing the nursing, and supplying all the conditions that have become known to him, for the recovery of the sick. Because his mode of expression is different from that of the New Zealander and Hebrew, is it therefore not true prayer? They both in praying did what they believed to con-

---

[11] Origin of Civilization and Primitive Condition of Man.

duce to the fulfillment of their prayer. So does
he. And he believes just as truly and fully as
they that it is God who answers the prayer, and
trusts and depends upon him as much as they;
only with a more intelligent trust, a faith into
which more of knowledge enters, and which
therefore is all the truer and firmer.

It would be a great mistake, however, to conclude from this that the expression of prayer in
thought and words had no value. It is not only
legitimate in all prayer, but necessary in most;
and in some it is the only expression possible or
needed.

In the first place, it is legitimate because it is
natural. "Out of the abundance of the heart
the mouth speaketh." The evolutionist would
say that speech is in the line of least resistance,
and therefore the very first direction in which
any deep and intense longing will discharge itself. At all events, we know that every such
desire will first of all express itself in speech.
And as the motor-force of prayer is one of the
deepest and strongest of all desires, it necessarily
follows the same law. And it does this as often as not without expecting or waiting for an
answer. Of this nature is nearly all ejaculatory
prayer. But it is not confined to this kind.
There is no kind of prayer whatever, where, if
the longing be strong enough, its first expression will not take the form of petition in words.
And even where not articulately uttered, the

want and desire will yet shape itself into some kind of a mental representation.

The necessity for this lies not only in the need of the surcharged nerves finding relief in this manner, but also in the circumstance that a prime element of prayer is its motive power, which is an important agency in the prayer's fulfillment. In order to give the motive a direction in accord with the dictates of reason and experience, its aim and end at least must be definitely conceived by the mind; which can only be done by a mental representation. By this our vague longing is defined and made clearly known to us, so that we can find and adopt the means for its accomplishment; or, just as likely, will see that our desire is not legitimate, is contrary to the divine order of being, and so can check it. Thus, the longing for revenge springs up in my breast. It is instantly put into definite form, or even into words. If I were a savage I would pray for vengeance on my enemy. But as it is, I at once recognize the emotion as opposed to the divine law, and instead of letting it come to fruition in a prayer, I quickly suppress it. Or, again, I have an indefinite but painful feeling of distress. The very effort to express this in words of petition defines, perhaps locates, the pain, gives me a clearer idea of my want, and enables me to see and apply the means for its removal. So that my first beginning to pray in words makes me continue the prayer in deeds, by which the fulfillment is brought about.

No special prayer could ever be accomplished if it were not first represented in thought, and thus the end clearly perceived, the motive strengthened and intelligently directed, and the means properly chosen and adjusted. Thus words, in the beautiful language of Dr. Mc-Cosh, "while forming no essential part of the prayer, will yet essentially aid it, by keeping the mind from falling into blankness and vacuity, by instigating and guiding it in a certain train—in short, they furnish cords to bind the sacrifice to the altar, they supply a censer in which the delicate incense of our feelings may be presented before the Lord." [12] Hence the very mental or verbal expression becomes an essential means in the answer to prayer.

This is still more directly and manifestly the case in prayer for purely spiritual benefits. There the mental exercise, strengthened by utterance in words, "contains within itself its own answer." In a fever of excitement and an agony of distress on account of the vivid sense of sinfulness that has been aroused, a soul gives vent to its feeling in a flood of vehement, burning prayer, "with strong crying and tears" perhaps. Gradually a calm settles over the storm-tossed soul; peace steals into the heart. Its

[12] Method of Divine Government.

fervent cries have been heard, and angels have come to minister unto it. The pent-up feelings found a vent and have exhausted themselves. The overstrained nerves discharged themselves in the very words and cries of the prayer. The whole system relaxes. There is a great calm. The prayer is answered; and not the less truly and really because by means of the very words and expression of the prayer itself. A young man comes and tells me how marvellously God always delivers him from temptation the moment he retires into his closet and betakes himself to earnest prayer. And I rejoice with him and am grateful; and not a whit less sincerely because I know that God answers his prayers by means of the prayers themselves, through the very act of his withdrawing himself from the tempting associations, of the mental bracing, and concentration of the attention needed for the formulating of his thoughts and wants and desires into words. He only knows that God fulfills his petitions. I know also how he does it. Both of us give to God alone the glory. There was a boy who was afflicted with a high, quick temper that often brought him into sore trouble and led to much evil. His good mother, who was very anxious about him, wisely advised him to make it a rule, whenever he should feel the first stirring of the angry passion, at once to retire to some private place and ask God to help him against his temptation. The boy did

so, and has grown up to be a strong, self-pos-
sessed man, of calm judgment and deliberate
actions. His prayers were heard and fully answered by that Supreme Being who has so con-
stituted the human mind that any sudden passion
may be diverted into another channel, may be
restrained, by the interposition of another motive or object calling the attention from it and
directing the discharge of the nerve-force
through other media. The boy's resolute check-
ing of his anger, and then discharging the feeling through the exercise of prayer, and his doing
this repeatedly and persistently, supplied the
conditions through which God fulfilled his petitions and cured him of his evil.

So it is when we pray for enlightenment,
peace, contentment, for any moral or spiritual
gifts, for which we cannot pray in deeds but
only in thoughts and words. The very framing
and utterance of the petition nearly always
bring its satisfaction. They are the divinely
ordered means for fulfilling prayer, and surely
bring as real and true an answer as is brought
in other spheres by other means. Nor can I see
why the knowledge of the means should in any
wise detract from the earnestness and sincerity
of the prayer, as some hold that it would. So
long as man has wants which he knows God
can and will supply, so long man will pray, regardless of his knowledge or ignorance of how
God does it. Nay, his knowledge that the sup-

ply depends upon conditions himself must furnish will only make him more earnest and diligent in complying with this necessity in order to have his wants more surely satisfied.

Need I yet show that the view of prayer which we have found so fully sanctioned by the principles of Evolution accords also as fully with the principles of the New Testament religion? Surely this will not be necessary. It must already be evident to all thoughtful readers of the Scriptures. The whole spirit of Christianity is one of self-renunciation, subjection to God, absorption in him. Its constant endeavor is to rid us more and more completely of everything that does not harmonize with him; to put off the old man entirely and put on the new; that it may no longer be we that live, but Christ that liveth in us; to make him all in all. Its whole heart is expressed in these words uttered by its Founder at the beginning of his ministry, "Thy will be done on earth as it is in heaven," and reiterated at its close, "Not my will, but thine be done!" Subjection to the Father, complete, absolute; union with him in thought and feeling and will; to work his works, to live his life, this is the innermost, deepest, and most permanently abiding longing and desire of every true Christian. It is the ultimate aim of all his life, even if not ever present in his consciousness. It must be the really central purpose and ruling motive of all his prayer. Not that God should change or modify his divine ways to suit man; but that he might instruct, guide, and direct man more wholly and fully to adapt himself in all his ways and being to God. True humility and unselfish devotion know no other prayer.

It is true, there may often, and often does, spring from the lips the cry of pain and petition that the cup of suffering be removed. But it is only the writhing of the human nature strained in the effort of adjustment to the divine; it is the discordant groan wrung from the harpstring as the Master turns the key to bring it into fuller tune and harmony. The next moment his hand sweeping gently over it is answered by a strain of heavenly melody as it rings out clear and strong, "Nevertheless, not as I will, but as thou wilt!" The heart is itself again. Its superficial emotion is gone. Its own abiding sentiment and perpetual prayer is again uttered; and once more it is satisfied. The divine has not been shifted. The cup is still held to the quivering lips. But the human has been conformed more fully to it. The quivering of the lips is from eagerness now, and not with terror; the heart throbs with gladness, in joyful strength, and not with the weakness of fear. With a mighty cry of triumph the bitter cup is drained. The man is dead. God lives alone. Captivity has been led captive. All things been put under his feet.

And how can we obey the commands that "men ought always to pray," to "pray without ceasing," and "continue instant in prayer," if prayer is nothing more than a request, a petition expressed in thought or words? Interpreting the words of Scripture in the light of the actions and life of the Saviour, it appears quite plain to me that Christian prayer is something very far removed from

" That drony vacuum of compulsory prayer
  Still pumping phrases for the Ineffable,
  Though all the valves of memory gasp and wheeze," [18]

which too frequently is substituted for it in the world. Its form and mode of expression seem ever to be regarded as of most consequence; its spirit as a matter of entire indifference. They vary infinitely. But "it is the same spirit that worketh in all." That is the alone essential thing. And that is nowhere shown to be a mere fitful and momentary up-flashing of superficial emotion; but always a deep-seated, all-absorbing, and continuous sentiment or principle; so deep and broad as to involve the whole character, as to be indistinguishable from the essential spirit of Christianity itself; a tendency of the whole being. He whom this possesses cannot but "pray without ceasing." Not alone in thought and words will it find expression; but

---

[18] Lowell—The Cathedral.

in the activity of every faculty and power of
mind and body. It will indeed often move his
lips to utterances of praise and petition; but as
often also will it move his hands and feet.
Even as, embodied in Christ, it made his whole
life one long prayer, so in every one in whom
Christ lives will it impel to the constant upward
look of faith, and trust, and obedience to him
whose wise and beneficent laws guide and direct
it. It will pray with the reason to find out and
understand his wonders more. It will pray with
the feelings, to hate and shun what opposes him,
to admire, love, and rejoice in whatever works
together with him. It will pray with the mus-
cles, to aid the working of his forces in the world
around, according to his marvellous order and
laws, to bring its own self, body, soul, and spirit
into full harmony, unity, with him who doeth
all things well.

Such I conceive to be true Christian prayer,
taught by the principles of the Bible and those
of Evolution alike. Not words alone; nor only
deeds. But both. Simply Christian life. A
consistent Godward striving of the entire being
of man. Such prayer it is of which the promise
stands forever true and sure, "If ye abide in me,
and my words abide in you, ye shall ask what
ye will, and it shall be done unto you;" and of
such prayer it is even more than a promise; it is
the glad verdict not only of the beloved disciple,

5

but of every true Christian's experience, which is expressed in the words, "whatsoever we ask, we receive of him, because we keep his commandments, and do those things that are pleasing in his sight."

V.

MAN.

"And the Lord God formed man of the dust of the ground, and breathed into his nostrils the breath of life; and man became a living soul." (GEN. 2: 7.)

"Howbeit that was not first which is spiritual, but that which is natural; and afterward that which is spiritual. The first man is of the earth, earthy."

(I COR. 15: 46, 47.)

"We must acknowledge, as it seems to me, that man with all his noble qualities . . . . still bears in his bodily frame the indelible stamp of his lowly origin."

(CHARLES DARWIN—*Descent of Man.*)

"Their keen necessities,
To ceaseless action goading human thought,
Have made earth's reasoning animal her lord;
And the pale-featured sage's trembling hand
Strong as an host of armed deities."

(COLERIDGE.—*Religious Musings.*)

"No one is more strongly convinced than I am of the vastness of the gulf between civilized man and the brutes; or is more certain that whether *from* them or not, he is assuredly not *of* them."

(THOMAS HUXLEY—*Man's Place in Nature.*)

"In the whole evolution God is the Alpha and the Omega; it comes from God, it reveals God, and at last brings forth beings who rising out of unreasoning nature know God and, distinct from him in being, reunite themselves to him by faith and love in the unity of a moral system."

(SAMUEL HARRIS—*Philosophical Basis of Theism.*)

"Whether the first of human kind were created outright, or, as the second narrative in Genesis represents it, were formed out of inorganic material, out of the dust of the ground, or were generated by inferior organized beings, through a metamorphosis of germs, or some other process,—these questions, as they are indifferent to theism, so they are indifferent as regards the substance of biblical teaching."

(GEO. P. FISHER—*Grounds of Theistic and*
Christian Belief.)

V.

MAN.

OF any ten persons whom you might ask what they understood to be the distinctive feature of the philosophy of Evolution, I suppose nine would at once answer, "The theory that man is descended from a monkey;" or as the Rev. Dr. Talmage is reported elegantly to have expressed it in a sermon, "Away back in the ages, my ancestor, they say, was an ourang-outang, a tadpole, or a pollywog; and it took a million years to evolute me!" Even if this were true, I do not see why it should ever have aroused so much opposition and holy horror in the minds of men; especially not why it should have done so in the minds of religious men, who have always been acquainted with the declarations of Scripture on the subject; unless indeed it be, as Frances Power Cobbe thinks, on account of "the special Semitic contempt for the brutes, which has unhappily passed with our religion into so many of our graver views." [1] Laying aside all prejudice in the matter, I can fully agree with Mr. Darwin when he declares, "For my own part, I would as soon be descended from that

---

[1] Darwinism in Morals.

heroic little monkey, who braved his dreaded enemy in order to save the life of his keeper; or from that old baboon, who, descending from the mountains, carried away in triumph his young comrade from a crowd of astonished dogs,—as from a savage who delights to torture his enemies, offers up bloody sacrifices, practices infanticide without remorse, treats his wives like slaves, knows no decency, and is haunted by the grossest superstitions;" [1]—if only, as Mr. Beecher said, I am far enough away from this ancestry!

But the popular identification of Evolution with "the theory that man is descended from a monkey," is wholly incorrect. Doubly so. For, in the first place, no evolutionist of any intelligence ever proposed or held such a theory. What the late Mr. Darwin maintained was, not that man was developed from any of the present species of apes, nor from any other form of animal now existing in the world; but that "man is an offshoot from the Old World Simian stem," some ancient extinct group of beings, from which, through the laws of variation and natural selection, a man-like creature was gradually derived, as at another time, by the same laws, an ape-like animal was produced. The former was the progenitor of the human race; the latter of the race of monkeys. Mr.

---

[1] The Descent of Man.

Darwin expressly warns us against falling "into the error of supposing that the early progenitor of the whole Simian stock, including man, was identical with, or even closely resembled, any existing ape or monkey." [3] Man, therefore, according to this theory, was no more derived from what we now know as monkeys, than these were derived from man. Both sprang from some other, earlier, now extinct form of being.

In the second place, this hypothesis of the development of man, solely by natural selection, is held by comparatively a few only of the leading evolutionists; and is not by any means among the most important or distinctive teachings of Evolution, nor one vitally affecting the validity of its principles. So long as evolutionists like Prof. St. George Mivart refuse to be Darwinists, or like Mr. Wallace are convinced of "the insufficiency of Natural Selection to account for the development of man," and believe in the existence of an "unknown higher law, beyond and independent of all those laws of which we have any knowledge," [4] so long Darwinism cannot be regarded as a vital part of the system of Evolution, and it must be granted that a man may be a consistent evolutionist without being in any way a Darwinist.

All that the principles of Evolution do require one to believe is that the coming of man upon

---

[3] The Descent of Man.
[4] Natural Selection.

the earth was not an exception to the general
method of the universe, but was in accordance
with the same; that, therefore, man was not
specially and miraculously created by an instantaneous act, and in the full possession of all his
organs and faculties as we now see him, but
that he was developed from previously existing,
lower, orders of being, and then grew and perfected his distinctively human nature until he
attained to his present highly organized physical
and mental condition, according to the same
order that is observed everywhere else in nature.
This is the hypothesis, in its most general form,
to which we now turn our attention.

Nor need we again be reminded, I trust, that
it is not the correctness or incorrectness of
the hypothesis that we are here concerned with
so much as the consequences which, if correct,
it would have upon our religion.   Let us remember the wise words of Dr. Asa Gray, if I remember rightly, that "upon very many questions a
truly wise man remains long in a state of
neither belief nor unbelief, while your short-
sighted man is apt to be preternaturally clear-
sighted, and to find his way very readily to one
or the other side of every mooted question."

The problem of the origin of man is not one
that has yet been finally settled.   Nor is it one
upon which our religion in any way depends.
To prove this, that we can believe in God, the
Bible, and salvation by grace, just as fully

whether we accept the hypothesis of Evolution
or not, is mainly what I hope to make clear.
For there are thousands who believe that it is
the most probable theory yet propounded; and
still they are told over and over again that it is
directly opposed to the Christian doctrine on the
subject. They therefore, at least many of
them, cleave to the former and forsake the latter. While many more think that because of
this theory Christianity itself is tottering. Personally I believe in the derivation of man from
lower forms of being; but I believe just as
firmly in the truth and saving power of my religion; and my earnest desire is to convince others,
as fully as I am convinced, that the doctrine of
human development does not oppose the teachings of Scripture, but rather makes them more
easily credible and intelligible.

The first thing the Scriptures affirm in the
matter is that "God formed man." I am aware
that for a long time this very general statement
was by many assumed to mean that man was
manufactured something after the manner in
which sculptors manufacture their clay models.
But this is now everywhere acknowledged to
have been a mere groundless assumption, alike
unworthy of rational beings and degrading to
the Christian idea of the Godhead. To hold it
would involve us in all manner of contradictions
and insuperable difficulties. It had to be abandoned even long before any other worthy ex-

planation had been found to put in its place.[5]
And it is now universally acknowledged that all
that the Scriptures do is to declare the fact,
"God formed man," without vouchsafing any
explanation whatever as to how he did it, by
what method, and in what time. They do,
however, say that he did not create him out of
nothing, but, so far at least as his physical nature is concerned, formed him out of pre-existing
materials, lower in the scale of existence than
man himself; while of his higher nature, his soul,
it is said, God "breathed into his nostrils the
breath of life;" which latter expression I think
every one allows to be clearly poetical and
figurative. To understand it as baldly litéral
would be to attribute a physical frame, with
lungs and other bodily organs, to God who is
pure Spirit. It is needless to say that this would
be impious presumption and contradictory of the
rest of the Bible.

But first let us confine ourselves to the first
part of the text, the general statement that

---

[5] I am glad to quote in this connection the latest words
of Dr. McCosh on the subject: "No difficulty arises on the
theory of development, which does not meet us on the
theory of the immediate creation of every new individual
and species. The works of nature are equally the works
of God on the one supposition as on the other, and the
mysteries bear against God in the one case as in the other.
The difficulties are swallowed up by the overwhelming evidence which we have in behalf of the omniscience and be-
nevolence of God."—*The Religious Aspects of Evolution.*

"God formed man." Does the theory of Evolution deny this? I maintain that there was never a scientific or philosophical theory that more positively agreed with it. Not only so; but it proves its truth, and insists on it as an absolute necessity. Deny it, and you deny the first principles of Evolution as well as the declaration of Scripture. There never was a more decided and weighty Amen uttered than Evolution gives to this sentence of Revelation.

We saw in a former Study that Evolution insists on a First Cause, "without whom was not anything made that was made." For it does not give any sanction to the deistic notion, held by many theologians, that this First Cause made the universe as the watch-maker constructs a watch, winds it up, and then lets it run on without supervision or activity on his part. The Absolute Power of Evolution and the God of the Bible alike are present everywhere, at all times, and actively potent in every movement and every manifestation of force, whether it be the springing of the blade of grass under our feet, or the elemental storm that rushes through the fiery surface of the sun; whether it be in directing the course of a mote of dust drifting in the air, or in guiding the endless journeys of a million worlds through the trackless expanse of space. Our "poet of nature" was as scientifically correct as he was religiously devout when in the forest's shade he sang,

"Father, thy hand
Hath reared these venerable columns, Thou
Didst weave this verdant roof. Thou didst look down
Upon the naked earth, and, forthwith, rose
All these fair ranks of trees. They in thy sun
Budded, and shook their green leaves in thy breeze,
And shot toward heaven." [6]

Nothing is uncaused; and God is the Cause of all causes. It is therefore no more blasphemous atheism than it is unscientific folly to deny that "God formed man." Whatever difference there may be supposed to exist between Scripture and Evolution, it certainly is not upon this point.

And this is fully and freely acknowledged by nearly all intelligent and fair-minded theologians and evolutionists alike. Says Dr. Samuel Harris, for instance, of the origin of man according to the process of Evolution, "The fact that it was a process which occupied time however long, and proceeded according to the laws and by means of the energies of an already existing nature, does not make it the less a work of God." [7] And the late Dr. Diman declared that "To hold that Mr. Darwin's theory affects in any way the proof of the existence of a Supreme Being, is an absurd misconception." [8] Indeed, Mr. Darwin himself, to say nothing of men like Mivart and Wallace,

---

[6] Bryant—A Forest Hymn.
[7] Philosophical Basis of Theism.
[8] The Theistic Argument.

repeatedly speaks of the direct agency of "the Creator" in the development of man as of the rest of the universe; while the ablest represent- ative of Evolution in this country, Prof. John Fiske, insists on the same as strenuously as the most orthodox theologian could, and declares that, while "Darwinism may convince us that the existence of highly complicated organisms is the result of an infinitely diversified aggre- gate of circumstances so minute as severally to seem trivial or accidental; yet the consist- ent theist will always occupy an impregnable position in maintaining that the entire series, in each and every one of its incidents, is an immediate manifestation of the creative action . of God."[*]

When we come to examine the supposed difference, we find that it is not between Script- ure and Evolution themselves, but between what some evolutionists on the one hand, and some religionists on the other, have gratuitously im- posed upon them, what they have fancied them to teach. Thus, the Bible account was assumed to mean that God created man, if not out of nothing, yet instantaneously, and in the full possession of all his perfect qualities. With such an assumption indeed Evolution does not agree. But what right has any one to make it? There is no ground or warrant for it anywhere.

---

[*] Darwinism and Other Essays.

The Bible neither teaches nor implies anything of the kind. On the contrary, it does clearly affirm not only that " God formed man," but that he " formed man of the dust of the ground," that is, out of already existing, inferior materials; therefore, not out of nothing, nor by an instantaneous fiat, but by some process, though it does not tell us by what process.

In so far, then, there is no contradiction, but a plain and positive agreement between Revelation and Evolution: Only the latter goes further and is more specific than the former. What the former says nothing about, but may imply, the latter seeks to explain. It says, "According to my principles this process was the same as that we see going on in other spheres of nature;" that is, by the agency of the mechanical, chemical, vital and other forces, acting according to their proper laws, and thus developing the inorganic "dust of the ground" until organic matter could appear; this until sentient creatures could arise; and then this, through variation and the different other modes of natural selection, and probably yet other processes, until human beings came into existence. How can this be said to contradict the Scriptural account? The latter tells us only the fact *that* God made man out of inferior material. Evolution tries to tell us *how* he did this. The two so far cannot be said to come into any kind

of conflict whatever. It is simply as if one had
said, "That house is made of wood;" and another had replied, "Yes, and I will tell you how.
First they cut down some trees; then they cut
them into scantling and boards; then they
fitted and nailed them together to form the joists
and floors and doors and window-frames, etc."
Would any one be foolish enough to say that the
second of these denied or contradicted the first?
On the contrary, it explains it, and makes it
more intelligible and capable of being realized
and understood. Just as little, then, can Evolution in so far be said to contradict Revelation.
It only makes us better able to understand and
form a clear conception of the latter. At all
events, no one need be afraid to go at least so
far as Dr. Fisher in feeling that, "Whether the
first of human kind were created outright,"
or formed through the process of Evolution,—
"These questions, as they are indifferent to
theism, so they are indifferent as regards the
substance of Biblical teaching." [10]

But even while doing this, and granting, like
Dr. McCosh, that man's "lower nature, and
especially his body, may have been formed out
of existing materials, it may be by secondary
causes," [11] there yet seems to many as to him to
be something further and different meant by

---

[10] Grounds of Theistic and Christian Belief.
[11] Christianity and Positivism.

the second part of the text of Genesis before us.[12]
Even if God "formed man of the dust of the
ground" according to the method of Evolution,
does not the added assertion, "and breathed into his nostrils the breath of life, and man became a living soul," imply that God also did
something more? There does seem to be some
distinction intended here. What is it? What
is the fact meant to be expressed by this figurative language?

It certainly does not mean that his physical
nature he received from the lower animals without God's agency, while his spiritual was, on the
contrary, imparted by God. The divine power
and activity were equally displayed in both gifts.
God gave us our bodies just as much as our
souls. Ultimately both are of the same origin.
Both are alike sacred and God-given. To try
to exalt the one at the expense of the other is
not only unwarranted by Scripture and science;
but is derogatory of the only true idea of God
and his agency in the world. Nor do I see that
the words necessitate us to assume any essential
difference in the manner and method of giving
the two parts of man; for instance, to suppose

---

[12] "I am not satisfied when I find myself and my friends
represented as mere developments from homogeneous matter, produced by differentiation. But I am willing to accept his [Spencer's] generalizations so far as the physical
powers of nature are concerned."—*Realistic Philosophy*,
vol. i.

that while the one was given derivatively, the other was imparted directly and immediately. I do not believe that there is any suggestion intended in the language of even so much of a reference to methods as to imply that there were different methods employed. The distinction is one referring primarily, if not only, to a difference in the results, the parts given, the physical and the spiritual natures of man, not to a difference of method at all.

That there is such a difference in the nature of man is recognized as clearly and as freely confessed by evolutionists as by theologians. Only the baldest materialists deny it. All others acknowledge it as radical and essential; though some differ as to the degree and importance of it. While men like Vogt, Büchner, and Haeckel of the Germans, hold that thought is only "a motion of matter," or, as it were, a secretion of the brain; others, like Lange, are confident of an impassable "gulf" between thought and brain-motions, and that "It will be forever impossible for science to find a bridge between these motions and the simplest subjective feeling of man."[18] So Prof. Tyndall declared in the preface to his famous Belfast Address, "When we endeavor to pass . . . . from the physics of the brain to the phenomena of consciousness, we meet a problem which

---

[18] History of Materialism, vol. 1.

transcends any conceivable expansion of the powers we now possess." Similarly Dr. Mayer says, "The brain is only the machine, it is not the thought. Intelligence, which is not a part of sensible things, cannot be submitted to the investigation of the physicist and the anatomist." [14] Mr. Wallace, too, has always held to an inexplicable and essential difference between man's physical and spiritual natures. To the testimony of these must be added that of Prof. Fiske, who, in one of his works, though speaking of "the wonderfully minute correlations between psychical action and brain.action which modern psychology is disclosing," yet emphatically declares that "it is utterly impossible that actions in the nervous system should ever, under any circumstances, stand in the relation of cause to psychical actions going on in the mind;" while he also assures us that "The doctrine of evolution, as applied by Mr. Spencer to the study of psychical phenomena, nowhere undertakes to interpret Mind as evolved from Matter." [15] At the same time, however, the words of Mr. Spencer himself are not always quite clear on this point. His teaching seems to be that, while there is no causal connection between physical and spiritual action, they both are "modes of the Unknowable," and are "transformable into each other." How such transformation takes place, he admits,

---

[14] Discourse at Innsbruck.
[15] Excursions of an Evolutionist.

is a mystery "which it is impossible to fathom,"
though "they are not profounder mysteries than
the transformations of the physical forces into
each other. They are not more completely beyond our comprehension than the natures of
Mind and Matter." [16]

The position of Evolution may, I think, be
summed up thus: Mind and matter, soul and
body, are two totally different phenomena; but
both the results of the one Absolute Power,
which manifests itself equally in both, though
in different ways. And this conclusion seems
to agree fully with the teaching of so orthodox
and profound a theologian and metaphysician
as President Noah Porter, who in other respects
seldom agrees with the doctrines of Mr. Spencer.
He says, in his "Human Intellect," that the
theory which "the progress of physiology in recent times, as well as the more careful study of
the conditions of certain of the psychical phenomena, have seemed to favor . . . . may
be stated thus: The force or agent which at
first originates the bodily organism, and actuates
its functions, at last manifests itself, as the
soul, in higher forms of activity, viz., in knowledge, feeling, and will. In other words, the
principle of life and of physical activity is one."

That part of man, therefore, which God
formed of "the dust of the ground," is the

---

[16] First Principles.

animal nature, his physical organs, instincts, appetites, and passions, which he has in common with lower forms of being. That part which God "breathed into his nostrils" so that he became a "living soul," consists of his spiritual faculties, like the higher reason and conscience, which distinguish him from all other creatures, and are of a higher order than, if not totally different in kind from, anything else known in nature.

How the soul was given to man can surely not be a question of vital import to religion. As a matter of fact, there is very little unanimity on the subject even among the leading evolutionists themselves, though they nearly all are at one as to the fact that it was by development, through the agency of the Absolute Power, that is, of God. Few indeed accept Mr. Darwin's view that natural selection was the sole mode of manifestation by which this Power did it; but even Mr. Wallace and his followers, who think that some time at the beginning of the tertiary period a new unknown power hastened and perfected the production of human intelligence, do not imagine that it was done otherwise than through secondary causes, and in accordance with the universal order of development. Mr. Darwin himself practically allows the possibility of this. For, while accounting for intelligence in man by the law of natural selection, when he comes to explain the origin of mind in the lowest animals, he has to confess that it "is as hopeless an inquiry as how life first originated;" and of this he speaks as "having been originally breathed by the Creator into a few forms or into one." [17]

That man, however, after having arrived at a certain stage in his development, should have been endowed with new and higher powers than any creatures below him possessed; and even that he should have received these from God through different agencies than any known before, is not in any wise contrary to the doctrine of Evolution; but rather in close analogy with other observed facts in the history of development.

Take, for example, the fact to which the words of Darwin just quoted refer. All scientific evolutionists are at one that in tracing life back and ever back to the lowest organisms, we come at last to a point where life stops, and where there is no conceivable connection with the inorganic matter below. No scientist of any standing to-day believes in abiogenesis, or what is popularly called spontaneous generation, that is, the production of living being from non-living matter by any known process. Prof. Huxley says on this point in his article "Biology," in the Encyclopedia Britannica, "The present state of knowledge furnishes us with no

---

[17] Descent of Man.

link between the living and the not-living;" while Mr. Tyndall wrote to the same effect in the "Nineteenth Century," holding "that no shred of trustworthy experimental testimony exists to prove that life in our day has ever appeared independently of antecedent life." How then are we to account for life? We can only do so by assuming some hitherto unknown mode of manifestation of the Ultimate Power, producing new combinations of its various phenomena, and resulting in life, or vital force, related, it may be, to chemical force and mechanical force, yet distinct from either, and superior to them in so far as it makes use of their products and agency in its own manifestations.

Similarly must we often confess our ignorance, if such it is, in following the course of the world. As far as scientifically demonstrable Evolution requires a new and before unknown form of power almost at each successive stage of the world's development, called into action by new requirements, new combinations and relations in the environment.

Before the lowest kind of life, vegetal, could appear, the elemental matter and forces had to be elaborated through myriads of centuries, and brought into such a condition that vegetables could absorb and be nourished by them. When this was done, then, and not before then, organic beings with vital powers sprang into existence, different from and superior to anything previously existing; depending indeed for their manifestation on the latter, yet using it, and even capable of raising it to their own level. When this had been done for centuries more, and vegetable matter had again been elaborated, its vital forces brought into more intricate adjustments, and its forms raised to a high state of organization, then, and not till then, animal life, a quite new and still higher manifestation of vital force, appeared. It could not have existed previously, as it can live only on organized matter. Then, finally, animal life had to develop for ages into ever higher and more complex forms, until the highest, the new spiritual power, the soul, was revealed, again depending upon all below it for its manifestation, yet itself superior to and acting upon it.

It will be noticed that this view, which perfectly accords with observed facts and with the principles of Evolution, as well as with the statement of Scripture, does away with the unreasonable idea had by many, that the soul was given to man as it were miraculously, that is, independently of all previous conditions and circumstances in man or outside of him, and without reference to any of the existing modes of force and being. And it also refutes the view of the materialist who would regard mind as only a form of matter, and spiritual phenomena as produced by physical causes. It recognizes clearly and fully the divine origin of the soul.

God made it. But he used matter and the lower modes of force to reveal it, used them as conditions of its manifestation; he acted through them. Therefore, he did not make man a living soul in any radically different manner from that in which he works always, and everywhere else; but according to an intelligible method and in harmony with the known order and laws of his being and operation. Certainly then Evolution does not contradict or oppose the declaration of Scripture, but on the contrary most fully substantiates and clearly explains the words, "The Lord God formed man of the dust of the ground, and breathed into his nostrils the breath of life; and man became a living soul."

Accept this view, and I do not see why the most orthodox believer and most strenuous evolutionist should not alike be ready to do so, and the doctrine of immortality follows naturally and necessarily. This Dr. Harris, who has recently elaborated a similar view in his work on the "Philosophical Basis of Theism," has clearly seen. "Once admit," he says, "that matter is perpetually passing through a process of evolution making it susceptible of being the medium of manifesting higher and higher powers, and the Scriptural doctrine of existence after death, and of the spiritual body, is accordant with this line of thought. To what extent the evolution may be carried and what higher powers it may become capable of revealing no one can pre-

dict." Yet even Evolution itself arouses the
questions within us that moved Empedocles on
Etna to exclaim,

> " To the elements it came from
> Everything will return.
> Our bodies to earth,
> Our blood to water,
> Heat to fire,
> Breath to air.
> They were well born, they will be well entombed!
>   But mind?. . . .
> And we might gladly share the fruitful stir
> Down in our mother earth's miraculous womb!
> Well might it be
> With what rolled of us in the stormy main!
> We might have joy, blent with the all-bathing air,
> Or with the nimble radiant life of fire!
> But mind—but thought—
> If these have been the master part of us—
> Where will *they* find their parent element?
> What will receive *them*, who will call *them* home?"

The Scriptures alone answer these questions
fully and explicitly, questions which not only
the heart but the reason asks. "The dust shall
return to the earth as it was, and the spirit shall
return unto God who gave it." Nor can it be
expected that Evolution should say anything
direct or definite about man's immortality. It
is a subject that is wholly without its sphere.
But for that very reason also it can and does
say nothing against it. At the same time from
its data and principles we may gather enough
indirect evidence to see that the weight of its
influence is all in favor of the doctrine of ever-

lasting life, and that there is nothing contained in them that need in the least shake the Christian's faith.

Not only is the general probability for it which Evolution affords strong, as Dr. T. T. Munger has beautifully stated it in one of his sermons, in which he says, "A living thing (like a flower) under the law of development comes to have a power of self-perpetuation that it did not have at first—why should it not be so with the life that has culminated in man? He is the flower of life, and in his heart alone may there be found the seed of eternal existence;"[18] but it seems to me that its fundamental law, that upon which the entire system is built, the law of the Persistence of Force, positively demands belief in some form at least of existence after death. According to it, as we have seen already, not a particle of force can ever be lost or annihilated; though its forms of manifestation may change almost indefinitely. "The life of man," says Dr. Carpenter, "or of any of the higher animals, essentially consists in the manifestation of forces of various kinds, of which the organism is the instrument."[19] Destroy the organism, and these forces simply have to manifest themselves in some other way. But not one of them is destroyed. They exist as really

---

[18] The Freedom of Faith.
[19] The Correlation and Conservation of Forces.

and actively as ever, only that they use some
other instrument, and in other relations and
different combinations.

There hangs a cloud in the morning sky. It
has a certain amount of moisture in suspension.
Now it is dissolved as rain which falls in a million crystal drops to the earth. Would any one
say that even a particle of that moisture had
been destroyed? It has only changed its shape,
from a vapory cloud to watery drops, or to a
little brooklet running to the sea. I am such a
cloud; my life is the moisture. Whether I exist in bodily shape or suffer physical dissolution,
the life is not destroyed. And just as the sum
of the universal moisture is never increased or
diminished, but ever goes on in endless routine
of transformation, so is there never a change in
the absolute Power of whom my life is but one
of an infinite variety of manifestations going
on in an endless series through all the ages of
eternity.

And precisely so of the higher spiritual life,
which, under the conditions supplied by certain highly complex combinations of the vital
forces, manifested itself as reason, conscience,
will. You may kill me, and so destroy the conditions of its special manifestation; but you will
not diminish by one particle the eternal Power
that worked in and through me. You will
change its form, however. Removing the conditions upon which it depends for its action, it

will manifest itself no longer as thought or will, as faith or love, but as some other force in some other way. This is an ultimate dictum of Evolution. Not a particle of that which now makes up myself will ever be destroyed. But, as the Apostle says, "we shall all be changed."

In itself, however, there is not much in this general fact to satisfy

> "this pleasing hope, this fond desire,
> This longing after immortality,"

that stirs in every human breast. General indestructibility is not by any means synonymous with personal immortality. What man wants to know is whether he will exist after death as the same conscious person who existed before death. The Bible and his Christian consciousness say, Yes! Tennyson expresses but a universal sentiment when he says,

> "My own dim life should teach me this,
> That life shall be forevermore;
> Else earth is darkness at the core,
> And dust and ashes all that is."[20]

What does Evolution say on the subject? Is it true, as some would maintain, that, while a general indestructibility must be allowed, for this no one any longer denies, scientific philosophy necessitates us to rest content with this; that, if anything, it obliges us to think that, when the physical organs are dissolved, when

---

[20] In Memoriam.

nerves and brain have crumbled into dust, when that intricate adjustment and combination of forces, without which we never have any experience of spiritual life, have been destroyed, then the latter also must cease to exist, and conscious life come to an end? There are those who would have us believe that Evolution requires such a conclusion. I am glad to confess, however, that nowhere in its teachings can I find anything even to suggest such an inference. On the contrary, they do give full sanction to the words of Prof. Fiske, who declares that with the conclusion "that the complex web of human consciousness cannot survive the disintegration of the organic structure with which we invariably find it associated, I do not agree. It is a conclusion not involved in the premises, and is one which no scientific philosopher, as such, has a right to draw. It necessitates as complete a transgression of the bounds of experience as any theologian is ever called upon to make." [21]

And indeed, though we might wish Evolution to be more explicit and clear in the matter, so as not to be so easily misunderstood, and misrepresented, yet will we not blame it therefor so much as the faithless hearts of those who fill up its silence with their groundless suppositions and words of unbelief. Listening with the ear of

---

[21] Excursions of an Evolutionist.

faith ourselves, we may hear no distinct utterance indeed, yet a whisper, less didactic than prophetic, coming from its direction to us. Ever, O son of man, it seems to say, ever hath the great Cause led thee up, not down; from good to better, not to worse; trust him!

> "From lower to higher, from simple to complete,
> This is the pathway of the Eternal Feet;
> From earth to lichen, herb to flowering tree,
> From cell to creeping worms, from man to what shall be.
> This is the solemn lesson of all time,
> This is the teaching of the voice sublime."

Elemental forces are succeeded by chemical, chemical by vital; plant-life was developed into animal, not by losing any of its higher functions, but by having still higher ones added to it; animal-life was graduated into man, not by taking from him aught that the animal had, but by adding to it reason, conscience, personality. When finally man shall change his form of life, are we to suppose that this method will be reversed, that his highest characterstics will be taken from him? May, nay must, we not much rather believe, even according to the observed order of Evolution, that he will retain all these, his higher reason, his knowledge of good and evil, his whole personality, and again have added to them new and still higher functions and powers, of pure, eternal spirit? Man no longer, indeed, but angel instead! The Evolution of nature prophecies it. The Revelation of God declares it. Shall not we believe it, hope it, realize it? And though, according to Evolution and Revelation alike, "it doth not yet appear what we shall be; we know that when He shall appear, we shall be like Him; for we shall see Him as He is." "So when this corruptible shall have put on incorruption, and this mortal shall have put on immortality, then shall be brought to pass the saying that is written, Death is swallowed up in victory."

VI.

SIN.

"Sin is the transgression of the law."

(I JOHN, 3:4.)

"By one man's disobedience many were made sinners."
(ROM. 5:19.)

"I find then a law, that, when I would do good, evil is present with me. For I delight in the law of God after the inward man: But I see another law in my members, warring against the law of my mind, and bringing me into captivity to the law of sin which is in my members."
(ROM. 7:21—23.)

"This fleshhood . . . how as a soaked
And sucking vesture it can drag us down
And choke us in the melancholy Deep!"
(MRS. BROWNING—*Aurora Leigh*.)

"It is astonishing that the mystery which is farthest removed from our knowledge (I mean that of the transmission of original sin) should be that without which we can have no knowledge of ourselves. It is in this abyss that the clue to our condition takes its turns and windings, insomuch that man is more incomprehensible without this mystery than this mystery is incomprehensible to man."
(PASCAL—*Thoughts on Religion*.)

" Bahnlos liegt's hinter mir, und eine Mauer
Aus meinen eignen Werken baut sich auf,
Die mir die Umkehr thürmend hemmt!
Strafbar ershein ich, und ich kann die Schuld,
Wie ich's versuchen mag, nicht von mir wälzen!"
(SCHILLER— *Wallenstein*.)

"O wretched man that I am! who shall deliver me from the body of this death?"
(ROM. 7:24.)

VI.

SIN.

No attempts have ever succeeded, though, strange to say, some have been made, to convince man that there is no sin, or that it is not the great bane of the world, the great hinderance in its progress toward perfection. The dire fact is too deeply rooted in human consciousness, too clearly written, even in letters of blood, on the pages of human history, too poignantly felt in the daily experience of the human heart. Its hideous reality is too patent and palpable a fact; a fact known to the race as clearly as to each individual of the race. To-day we cannot go where sin is not. And in the remotest yesterday of the past its shadows still are seen, even deeper and blacker than now. The ancient chroniclers have inscribed its name upon their scrolls. The olden poets and seers have pictured its form in bold outline and vivid colors. While at the present day poets, historians, philosophers and theologians, still are unable to escape from its presence, or banish the dread specter from their pictures, their records, theories, and systems. Nor is there much difference between the oldest and the most modern definitions of what sin is. For each one's conscious-

ness agrees with that of all in defining it as conscious, voluntary disobedience to the divine law.
Yet there are those who would have us believe that the theory of Evolution in so far vio-
lates the testimony of human consciousness and
universal experience as to deny the essential
nature of sin.   They say it has destroyed the
freedom of the will, and therefore man's moral
character and accountability.   It is true, according to Evolution the human will cannot be free
as scholasticism defines freedom.   It is true, it
has shown conclusively that man is not the
"Great Exception" to everything else in the
world in being absolutely outside of all law, of
all those forces and influences, physical and
moral, by which the universe is governed.   But
it in no wise denies the freedom and accountability of man in the sense and to the extent
that this was done by most of the early Fathers
of the Church, to say nothing of Calvin,
Edwards, and a multitude of devout theologians
of but a few years ago.   Did these deny the
fact of sin and of the guilt of man?   On the
contrary, it was the one doctrine to which they
clung with seemingly the greatest fondness,
the one fact upon which they dwelt most continually and eloquently.   Evidently in them the
conviction of the reality and universality of sin
was not at all dependent upon the doctrine of
the freedom of the will; and we might share it
with them even though Evolution denied the

latter far more absolutely and emphatically than
it does.

Moreover, in showing that

" Evil its errand hath as well as Good,"

in the labor of the ages to bring forth the highest glory of God, Evolution does no more than
accept the simple fact of history and experience.
The Bible itself declares the same truth over
and over again, not only affirming that under
God "all things work together for good," but
rejoicing that even "the wrath of man shall
praise him." It by no means makes sin less
sinful to know, as none can help knowing,
that it has been and still is among the most
active and potent factors in the development of
the world, and that this development is ordered in such a manner that ultimately, in spite
of sin, aye, and by means of it, absolute and
eternal good shall be the result.

Evolution simply accepts sin as an incontrovertible fact, just as the Bible and theology do.
And no less than they does it hold it to be a
voluntary, conscious transgression of the moral
law of God, an offence against God. But it
tries also to show why it is such, and how.
When the little child asks, "Why is it wrong
for me to do this?" it is enough to answer,
"Because Father has forbidden it." But when
the full-grown man asks the question, he wants
a fuller answer, and has a right to it. This

Evolution endeavors to give. It says, "Because the Father has forbidden it, as it would bring harm to you and your fellow men and discord into the harmony of the all." Does it remove the guilt of sin, and our consciousness thereof, or the righteousness of its penalty, to know that sin is not an arbitrarily decreed thing, unaccountable and mysterious, but that its distinction from virtue is a distinction deep down in the nature of things, consequent upon the divine ordering of the universe, as this latter is consequent upon the very nature of the deity? Certainly not; as little as it destroys our reverence for God, and weakens our disposition to abide by his laws, to know enough of the why and how of these to be able to obey them with the full consent of reason, and not only with a blind, unreasoning obedience. And, fully granting the fact *that*, Evolution attempts no more than just this, to tell us somewhat of the *how* and *why*.

They are questions, indeed, that early disturbed the Christian Church. Already in the first few centuries men asked, Whence came sin into the world? How came it? What is the cause of its universality? Granted that the first man did sin, how could that affect all mankind after him? At the beginning of the fifth century the controversy, on this last point especially, had involved almost the entire Church, and itself caused more sinful bitterness, hatred,

cursing, and persecution than almost any other
question, with perhaps one or two exceptions.
And from the time of Pelagius, who maintained that Adam's sin had no evil effects on
the race except by the force of its example; and
of the great Augustine, who held that as Adam
had himself been the whole race, man as a
whole must have "sinned in Adam" and must
share his actual guilt; up to quite recent times,
theologians have been more or less violently
exercised in the matter. And theology alone
could never settle it. There are questions involved in it on which the Bible is simply silent;
and which metaphysics can never decide. It
was really left for Evolution to give to theology
a theory at least as rational as any before proposed, as fully in accord with Scripture itself,
and more fully verifiable by science than any
other.

It teaches that the tendency to sin is hereditary and universal; that man's unregenerate nature has inherited evil inclinations, seeds of sin,
that will inevitably lead him to the guilt of sin
unless his nature be in so far radically changed.
And this is substantially the view now virtually
adopted, or at least allowed, by most theologians; and seems fully to agree with the Bible.

As every other theory of original sin must, so
does this view, depend upon the fact of mankind having a common origin and nature. This
fact the Bible indeed both expressly declares,

when it makes Adam the progenitor of the whole race of man, and uniformly implies, everywhere taking for granted that God "hath made of one blood all nations of men." But it was strenuously denied in comparatively recent times by many prominent scientists, as by the late Prof. Louis Agassiz, who was regarded as a champion of Christianity by many. He affirmed that there must have been more than one original pair of human beings to account for the great differences between the several races of men. To reconcile this with Scripture sorely puzzled theologians. In fact, they could only do it by the most gratuitous assumptions, and grossest liberties with the sacred text; and even then they involved themselves in all manner of difficulties and inconsistencies.

Deny the unity of the race, and the whole scriptural doctrine of sin, as that of salvation, must be changed. But how was this unity to be established, over against the declarations of the leading authorities in science ? Theology was at a loss to know. Then came Evolution, and showed the old anthropology to have been wrong; fully substantiated and gave the strength of unity of plan and system to the many separate testimonies furnished by paleontology, archæology, comparative anatomy, philology, and theology; and proved conclusively that the Scriptures are scientifically correct. All men, white and black, red and yellow, are descended from one original stock; and their differences in color, anatomical structure, and mental characteristics, are only the results of variation, conditioned by their environment, the struggle for existence, and the influence of the various modes of natural selection.

In view of the fundamental importance of the doctrine of the unity of the race to Christian theology, the service rendered to the latter by the establishment of the doctrine on a firm scientific basis, cannot be overrated. For, as before said, the doctrine of human sinfulness depends directly upon it. The Bible everywhere makes it appear not only that our carnal nature is sinful, but that it is such in consequence of the sin of our first parents. But if the Negro had a different origin from us, and the Indian still a different one, and so every race is sprung from a different stock, then what makes them sinful? The first parents of each of them must have separately fallen. But the Scriptures tell us not a word about anything like this; while they imply and declare the opposite, expressly affirming that "through one man sin entered into the world."

As to how it did this, Revelation and Evolution coincide remarkably. The former, if we interpret its picturesque language of oriental poetry in the simplest way, tells us that when the first "man became a living soul," a self-determining person, it was revealed to him that

one course of action would be in accordance
with God's will, and another would not; and
that the latter would bring its penalty of misfortune with it. Then he deliberately chose
this course; he disobeyed God's clearly understood commandment. And by this he became
morally guilty, sinful; and he knew it. By
that act he formed for himself a sinful character;
whereas before his nature had been morally
guiltless, innocent and sinless. His sin, therefore, consisted in his consciously and voluntarily
violating divine law. For as the Apostle John
says, "Sin is the transgression of the law," that
is, the conscious, voluntary transgression.
Had Adam not known that God had forbidden
him to eat of that particular tree, he would not
have sinned, since, as Paul declares, "where no
law is, there is no transgression." This, then,
is the scriptural account of the origin of sin.

Now mark what Evolution tells us. According to it, as was seen in our last Study, there
was a time when man had not yet come into
possession of the higher powers, called soul;
was not conscious of himself as a morally responsible person. He was simply an animal
and no more. Sin was therefore impossible for
him then. But in his upward development he
at length arrived at a state in which he became
conscious of a Supreme Being, and of himself
as related to this Being. At the same time he
recognized certain modes of action as being ac-

cording to the will of the Supreme Being, and others as opposed to it; he became conscious of right and wrong, good and evil, and of the obligation to do the one and avoid the other. The moment this point in what Mr. Spencer calls "that grand progress which is bearing humanity onward to a higher intelligence and nobler character" was reached, man became a moral agent. He was no longer a mere animal, but a "living soul;" and, according to Milton's description, than all other creatures

> " Of far nobler shade, erect and tall,
> Godlike erect, with native honor clad,
> In naked majesty, seemed Lord of all,
> And worthy seemed; for in his looks divine
> The image of his glorious Maker shines." [1]

This stage in his evolution corresponds with the time when, according to Genesis, God revealed to Adam as his divine law, from what trees in Eden he might eat, and from which he might not. When now man deliberately disobeyed this law, chose what he knew to be wrong in preference to the right, he fell from his potential state of perfect righteousness; sin entered into the world.

As in the accounts of the origin of man, so here again we see that there is no real opposition between the scriptural account of the origin of sin and that to be inferred from the the-

---

[1] Paradise Lost.

ory of Evolution. The latter merely explains the former. The essential facts in both are the same. The main reason, probably, why men have so commonly failed to see this agreement lies in the fact that the writer of Genesis has presented his account in such a form and manner as to make it appear as though the development from bare animal to man as moral agent had been a single instantaneous act; he passes over the indefinitely many steps in the graduation, and dwells only on the result, the culmination of the process; while Evolution, being specially concerned with the process itself, traces it as minutely as it can in all its various stages. It is less interested in the final fact that man did discern God, and recognize himself as related to him, than in the method by which he attained to this. Hence it chiefly emphasizes the *how*, and tries to show it as clearly as possible. How did God first make himself known to our manlike progenitor? it asks. How did this creature first learn to know God? And to recognize his law? And to realize his obligation to obey it? And, then, why did he disobey it after he had arrived at this stage of moral responsibility?

That individual evolutionists in trying to answer these questions should differ very widely in their details, is probably not to be greatly wondered at where there are so few positive data on which to base their views. It is enough that nearly all agree on what, indeed, the principles of Evolution demand, that the primitive man was not at once endowed with a full and true conception of God, but that he received this gradually, at first in an exceedingly crude form, and mixed with much that was erroneous. With a mind lower and more shallow than that of the lowest barbarian now living, he could apprehend but a very little of the Truth at a time, catch only here and there, now and then, a mere glimpse of the divine Light. Perhaps here only the idea of invisible being, taught him through his dreams. Or there the truth of an unseen Power, suggested by disease or a storm. Straightway indeed this idea, the little grain of truth, was invested with all manner of false notions, was accompanied by, almost lost in, the belief in ghosts, witches, and the low faith and practices of fetichism. But yet it is there: the recognition of invisible existence and superhuman agency in the world. Probably, like the pearl hidden under the rough shell and in the ugly slime of the oyster, this little grain had to have such a gross, material setting, else would half-brutal man never have found it at all; and had to be so abused, else would its true polish and beauty never have been laid bare. So low is the idea, however, that we scarcely are willing to call it a recognition of God. Him whom we love and adore, from whom we are unable to dissociate the conception of infinite power, wisdom and beneficence, it saw only as dreadful, to be feared, or if possible outwitted or overcome.

Perhaps after a while our primitive ancestor notices how the powers that he so dreads are after all not exclusively evil and destructive. He marks how the sun not only fiercely burns and blisters him in summer, but also kindly warms him in winter. The mighty torrent not only dashes his raft to pieces, but also gives him its fish for food, and bears him on its bosom from place to place. He begins to worship seen and unseen objects of power not only as evil, but also as good. Then, still further, as the human mind grows, experience is gathered, and thought begins to stir, even while still worshipping natural objects, it commences to discern an unseen immaterial power behind all these. The principal deities are no longer residents of the earth, but denizens of the air, of a spirit-world all their own. In the words of Schiller,

> " To yon starry world they now are gone,
> Spirits or Gods that used to share this earth
> With man as with their friend;"

and they can be approached only through certain favored mediums, shamans. If this degenerated into the worship of these shamans themselves, and then was transformed into image-worship, and polytheism, the processes by which

it came to pass are not difficult to see; nor that
it would serve to add new and precious rays of
the divine Truth that so laboriously man was
trained to behold. For, whatever the steps in
the progress, it must have been slow, and by
many devious ways. Only the patience and
wisdom of an infinite Father could have brought
it to the stage in which we ourselves are
found, and which presumptuously we are apt to
think of as the stage of final perfection, when
perhaps even we are as yet standing but in the
dim dawn of the morning, seeing only as
"through a glass, darkly;" imagining, fancy-
ing far more than we really discern, and too
often blaming those who cannot see as we think
we see, and quarreling idly with them.

By some such process as this, Evolution supposes, man was first taught to apprehend the
Divine, and gradually to see more and more of
him, and more clearly and truly. Not that
he was not always revealed, as is the air or the
blue sky. But our primitive forefathers could
not see him as we see. Their spiritual vision
had first to be fashioned through the ages so as
to be able to discern him. Yes, truth, the
spirit's atmosphere, filled space from all eternity.
But man, like a little plant sprung from the
darkness and the dust, though living, moving,
and having his being in it, could but absorb so
much as his earthy mind would hold; a little at
a time, until he grew in strength and size to

be a mighty tree, that rears its top high up, and feels Truth's gentlest breeze that erst with all its sweetness far out of reach had passed. If he thus was made to grow through material means, even through means we now despise, does it not only the more marvelously illustrate the wisdom, power, and infinite beneficence of that Being who was the divine Agent in this wondrous work?

It will be remarked and probably thought strange that, according to the view given, the apprehension of God was induced and developed without any reference to moral law and obligation. In our minds the idea of right and truth are so intimately connected with the idea of God that we can scarcely conceive of their separate existence. Yet according to nearly all evolutionists, however much they differ as to other details, the development of moral conceptions was not coincident with the growth of the consciousness of God. The idea of right, and conviction of duty, came later than the idea of deity, and at first quite independently of it. And this seems to be substantiated by the observed fact that, even at the present day, there still are savages whose religion has not a single ethical element in it. Indeed we would hardly expect it to be otherwise. The moral attributes of God are his highest, least physically palpable. The lowest mind could not perceive them. They are too lofty and spiritual. Such minds had to be educated and trained to a considerable degree before they could be capable of seeing beyond his power and might and be made to behold his goodness and truth. And this would again be done by leading man gradually from low to higher, from grosser to more refined, through such carnal means as the feelings of pleasure and pain, the experiences of power and authority, of usefulness and profit, and of obligation to his fellow men.

In other words, by a long series of "beneficent adaptations" of the as yet only half-human nature of primitive man to his environment, and of the latter to the former, brought about through the struggle for existence, the survival of the fittest, heredity, the family and social instincts, and all the other modes of natural selection and methods of divine government, his very instincts of self-preservation and self-preferment were made the instruments of his gradually being brought to recognize other than purely selfish ends of being.

To hold his own against the other beasts of forest and field, and against the fierce elements, he at first had to have recourse to cunning, deception, and craftiness of every kind. To overreach and rob them for his food, and kill them for clothing and in self-defence. Then he was brought to see that it was more profitable and conducive to his own good to live at peace and in alliance with the other creatures of his own kind than to rob and kill them. Society came into being, with ever more and more complex relations. Ever more and more he learned to restrain his selfish appetites and passions for the good of the community; because thus his own greatest good would be served. The process illustrates the truth expressed by Coleridge how, under the divine guidance,

" Self-love but serves the virtuous mind to wake,
As the small pebble stirs the peaceful lake:
The center moved, a circle straight succeeds,
Another still, and still another spreads,—
Friend, parent, neighbor, first it will embrace;
His country next, and next all human race;
Wide and more wide, th' o'erflowings of the mind
Take every creature in of every kind."

Thus did God patiently prepare incipient human nature, curbing and putting down the animal part, and leading up the spiritual until it was strong enough and ready for the manifestation of its highest power, the moral faculty. But this would not be done, properly speaking, before the idea of right and duty was integrally connected with the idea of God. "Nor would this take place," Sir John Lubbock thinks, "until the Deities were conceived to be beneficent beings. As soon, however, as this was the case, they would naturally be supposed to regard with approbation all that tended to benefit their worshippers, and to condemn all actions

of the opposite character." [2] Whether in this
particular way or not, we know that early in
the race's life it was made to see that it was
not only expedient and profitable for man to
restrain his envy, hatred, and revenge, refrain
from robbing his neighbor, and to do good to
his fellows, but that it was a law of God, and
on that account only was profitable; that right,
goodness, and truth have as their ultimate and
highest warrant simply the will of the divine
Being, and therefore alone must be followed,
even regardless of the merely secondary consideration of utility.

It was this element, however arrived at, that
was an essential agent in the perfecting of conscience as an inherent and authoritative power
of the human mind, and that helps to explain
the possibility of the process, as stated by Mr.
Spencer, by which "the experiences of utility organized and consolidated through all past generations of the human race, have been producing
corresponding nervous modifications, which by
continued transmission and accumulation, have
become in us certain faculties of moral intuition—certain emotions responding to right and
wrong conduct, which have no apparent basis
in the individual experiences of utility. [3]

In thus accounting for the human conscience,
every one must see at once that there is and

---

[2] Origin of Civilization and Primitive Condition of Man.
[3] Letter to J. S. Mill quoted in Bain's Moral Science.

can be no opposition between Evolution and the Scriptures. The latter say nothing about it;—though speculative theology may. They merely declare that God gave it to man, and "man became a living soul;" nothing about how he gave it. Evolution says, According to the observed method of divine manifestation in all other cases, it is most likely that this power was given gradually, after long preparation and patient training. As the earth was first prepared for the reception of vegetable life, and this prepared the way for animal, and then animal life had to be developed up into highly organized forms before the highest creature, the human, could be formed, so in this last, its whole organism had to be refined through a long experience before it was fit and able to recognize God and his law, and its own obligation to them.

Just as little contradiction is there, and even more explicit agreement, on the question of the validity and divine authority of conscience. Christian theology says, It is the voice of God. Evolution declares, in Herbert Spencer's words, "It is a mode of manifestation of the Unknowable; and having this for its warrant."

If we ask why certain modes of conduct are good and others bad, which invariably have good and bad results, the answer of both is simply that such is the nature and constitution of things which the divine Power has impressed upon them. Therefore we must do right without further question. Not as the utilitarian says, because it will conduce to our greatest happiness; but as the Christian is taught, and as Mr. Spencer declares, because certain divinely given fundamental laws of our being demand it, which "are to be conformed to irrespective of a direct estimation of happiness or misery." [4] Certainly nothing could be clearer than this. And that it is true and correct is by nothing more convincingly shown than by the very fact which the theory of the gradual evolution in man of the religious and moral instincts so clearly brings out, that the conscience is not a merely subjectively conceived notion, or a form of thought arbitrarily imposed by the fiat of a superior Power, but that it is a deep, ineradicable conviction derived through inherited experience, formed by the objective reality of the truths to which it testifies. The truth is true not because conscience tells us so; but conscience tells us because it is true. Right is right and to be done, good is good and to be followed, not for the reason that conscience says so; but it says so for the reason that it is so. Even as according to Evolution the eye has been gradually formed into the delicate and marvellous organ of sight by the influence of the light and the whole outer world upon the organism, thus

---

[4] Letter to J. S. Mill quoted in Bain's Moral Science.

giving the utmost possible certitude to the testimony of our vision, so the soul's eye, the moral convictions and sentiments, are but the inner impressions, deeply engraven on the human spirit by the action of the outer realities upon it.

According to this view, therefore, the very existence of the moral faculty is the highest evidence of its validity and divine authority. "For clearly," to quote the forcible and beautiful language of Prof. Fiske in his address on Evolution and Religion, "when you say of a moral belief or a moral sentiment that it is a product of evolution, you imply that it is something which the universe through untold ages has been laboring to bring forth, and you ascribe to it a value proportionate to the enormous effort that it has cost to produce it. Still more, when with Mr. Spencer we study the principles of right living as part and parcel of the whole doctrine of the development of life upon earth; when we see that, in an ultimate analysis, that is right which tends to enhance fullness of life, and that is wrong which tends to detract from fullness of life,—we then see that the distinction between right and wrong is rooted in the deepest foundations of the universe; we see that the very same forces, subtle and exquisite and profound, which brought upon the scene the primal germs of life and caused them to unfold, which through countless ages of struggle and death have cherished the life that could live more perfectly and destroyed the life that could live less perfectly, until Humanity, with all its hopes and fears and aspirations, has come into being as the crown of all this stupendous work,—we see that these very same subtle and exquisite forces have wrought into the very fibres of the universe those principles of right living which it is man's highest function to put into practice. The theoretical sanction thus given to right living is incomparably the most powerful that has ever been assigned in any philosophy of ethics. Human responsibility is made more strict and solemn than ever, when the eternal Power that lives in every event of the universe is thus seen to be in the deepest possible sense the author of the moral law that should guide our lives, and in obedience to which lies our only guarantee of the happiness which is incorruptible,—which neither inevitable misfortune nor unmerited obloquy can ever take away." **

I have dwelt upon this point in some detail, because it is the one most violently attacked by many as failing to make sin really sinful, and because it is necessary to the proper comprehension of the doctrine of original sin, which Scripture has always insisted upon, but theology too often failed to explain in rational manner.

** Excursions of an Evolutionist.

It is asserted even by writers like Miss Cobbe that according to such a theory of the origin of our moral faculty as is given by Evolution, "We may regret our *imprudence*, but it is quite impossible we should ever again feel penitence for a *sin*." It is spoken of as "supplying us at the utmost with a plausible theory for the explanation of our preference for some acts as more useful than others, but utterly failing to suggest a reason for that which is the real phenomenon to be accounted for,—namely, our sense of the sacred obligation of rightfulness, over and above, or apart from utility." [6]

There is force in these objections. When I see men deliberately sacrificing their reputation, their comforts, their health, their life itself out of noble loyalty to the Right, in simple obedience to the authoritative OUGHT uttered by a still small voice within their breast; when I hear the heart-rending groans of intense agony wrung by remorse for a wrong action from strong men who could be torn limb from limb by wild beasts without ever letting an expression of pain escape them;—I too feel that "the experiences of utility, organized and consolidated through all past generations of the human race," are inadequate to satisfactorily explain the facts. With Mr. Darwin I ask, "Why should a man feel that he ought to obey one instinctive feel-

---

[6] Darwinism in Morals, etc.

ing rather than another? Why does he bitterly regret, if he has yielded to the strong sense of self-preservation, and has not risked his life to save that of a fellow-creature?'" But Mr. Darwin's explanation satisfies me even less than Mr. Spencer's. The satisfaction and banishment of the temporary selfish instinct and return to consciousness of the permanent social one, does not account for all involved in the case. Nor does Sir John Lubbock's theory that authority is the origin, and utility the criterion, of virtue, seem to me to explain any better the facts to be accounted for.

While all these theories may serve to show us how the knowledge of right and wrong, of good and evil, was given to man in the ages-long training under God's hand, I am free to confess that, in themselves, they do not account for the existence, the authority, the power of the sense of duty and obligation, of guilt and sin, which accompany this knowledge. Inherited experience, association of ideas, authority, training,—all these may have helped; but there seems to me to have been something more needed to produce those "nervous modifications" which make virtue obligatory and vice a sin for us. These feelings, and they are more than ordinary feeling, seem to me to point to a closer, more vital and immediate,

---

¹ The Descent of Man.

connection between the absolute Right and Good One, and his reflections in the human spirit, than has yet been pointed out, or perhaps yet can be definitely traced. It takes long and patient culture and training till the ear and the eye are brought to recognize the harmony of sounds and of colors. But that stage once reached, and every tuneful chord, each beauteous blending tint, causes an answering thrill of joy in the soul, each discord a quiver of pain. It is different from the mere knowledge of what is correct. It is more than that. It is an addition to it. So may it have taken generations and long centuries of time to bring the human spirit to recognize its inner deep affinity with the divine. But once realized, from the very blending of the two, may not the OUGHT be but the sympathetic bond, the divine force that binds spirit to spirit, the thrill of harmony vibrating through both? And the deep sense of sin, the moral discord, the clash and the pain of rupture between them? OUGHT the force that draws and binds steel to magnet; SIN the violence that separates them, even while they strain for union.[8]

And, further, may not this fact, so intensely real as to belong to the very constitution of the universe, and yet so inexplicable as in itself to

---

[8] A very suggestive paper on "The Evolution of Conscience," by the Rev. F. H. Johnson, appeared in the Andover Review, vol. ii.

suggest some essential connection with the being and nature of him who is past finding out,—may not the imperative demands of duty and the pleasure of meeting the demand, as well as the painful guilt of disobedience, themselves be a faint foreshadowing, nay, an earnest, and actual foretaste of life in another, higher stage of existence? When there shall be no longer any material, fleshly hinderances to a complete, harmonious union between pure souls and the absolute Spirit, will not the still small voice, whose broken whispers even now are sweet as angels' kisses, break forth into a fullness of ecstatic joy stronger than any seraph's shout, glorious as the eternal music of the spheres, itself a note in the infinite harmony of the all? And if even now each temporary rupture of our soul from the Absolute, each single act of discord, brings the anguish of remorse to rend our heart, when that rupture shall have become permanent, that discord eternal,—what then?

But all mere speculation aside; whether we think that the evolutionists' theory of the origin of conscience and sin be correct, or whether we deem it inadequate, it does not in the slighest degree affect the Christian doctrine on the subject. If it does not fully account for all the observed facts, especially the emotional accompaniments of the moral judgments, this does not invalidate the entire theory. And we may ask, what theory on the subject does entirely satisfy the reason? Whereas if we do accept it, we have the assurance of the most thoughtful and devout theologians that our sense of right and wrong, of merit and sin, will not in the least be weakened thereby. "Whether the moral sense is a faculty implanted in man by a supreme intelligence," declares one from whom I have already quoted, "or whether the moral sense is the result of a long process of development which a supreme intelligence has designed and superintended, are questions which do not in the least affect the authority of conscience, or the validity of the distinctions which it shows." [*]

So long as the Bible and Evolution agree as fully as they do in holding sin to be a willful transgression of God's law, and conscience an authoritative voice from God which we ought to follow, there can be no conflict between them. The essential facts in the matter they equally acknowledge. It is only on the explanation of the facts that they differ; or rather, the Bible simply accepts the facts, and nothing more, while Evolution accepts the facts no less fully, but tries also to account for them. Whether we think that it succeeds in this or not, really makes very little difference.

---

[*] Diman—The Theistic Argument.

One thing, however, must I think be granted, that on no other theory than that of Evolution can the Bible teaching with reference to original sin be as naturally, rationally, and therefore satisfactorily explained. Why is it, if man was originally created in the full possession of his perfected spiritual, moral, faculties, that we yet, as Paul says, "see another law in our members, warring against the law of our mind, and bringing us into captivity to the law of sin which is in our members?" It seems impossible that the one act of transgression of our first parents should have been capable of so totally and permanently eradicating the original moral excellences, and warping all human nature forever, as we must believe if the first man was fully developed and completely equipped in body and soul.

According to Evolution, however, all this becomes plain. The "law in our members warring against the law of our mind" is simply our animal nature received from our brute ancestors. The same forces of heredity through which the innate power of conscience was formed and is transmitted, also transmit from generation to generation the selfish appetites, desires, passions, and mental habits that were engendered and so largely developed in the ante-human state of our race-existence. They are part of our earliest formed nature, derived by inheritance from our remote animal ances-

tors. What is the love of power and conquest
that leads nation to war against nation, and
shed the blood of thousands, but the self-same
motive, inherited from primitive man, that led
him and his companions with club and spear
to fall upon their weaker neighboring village,
to pillage its huts, and murder its inhabitants
or hold them in cruel slavery? A remnant of
the same disposition it is that makes men delight in military maneuvers and sham battles,
that gives a charm to perilous adventures, and
even a certain enjoyment to the reading at least
of glowing accounts of brutal prize-fights. The
tendency to gloat over a struggle and rejoice
with the stronger; the strange fascination which
scenes of bloodshed and cruelty still exercise
over many;—they are the relics in our carnal
nature of those primitive times when such
struggles and scenes were the necessary conditions of existence. What is the prevalence
of gluttony, drunkenness, immorality and adul-
tery, that shows itself in so many ways, open
and disguised, in modern society, but a proof
of the still potent influence of those bestial instincts that once dominated semi-human man?
And similarly in every individual do we see
the same illustrated. The animal greed that
was developed in the struggle for existence, and
then served a purpose, still shows itself, only
slightly modified, in the grasping disposition of
the child that quickly reaches for the largest

piece of cake on the table; in the senseless
avarice of the miser hoarding his shining gold;
and in the eager anxiety of the monopolist to
amass ever more and new millions. In these
the greedy tendency has no rational purpose.
They simply follow a blind, inherited inclination. So the instinct of self-preservation that
impelled man in the savage state to return blow
for blow, and to hunt his enemy to the death,
still shows itself in us, though no longer needed
for our own safety or for any other purpose, in
the anger we feel at any affront, the instinctive
disposition to return blow for blow and insult
for insult, the feeling of revenge, and the unforgiving temper displayed by too many.

All such feelings, emotions and sentiments of
selfishness, which spring from a regard for self
and have in view the preferment and advantage of self, are not considered sinful in brutes.
They know nothing higher, and have no obli-
gations to any higher law. But since

> " 'Tis the sublime of man,
> Our noontide majesty, to know ourselves
> Parts and proportions of one wondrous whole," [10]

since the higher life and law of right, goodness,
and truth have been revealed to us, obedience
to our former lower mode of life is sinful. God
has shown man a better way; led him into
new relations, to behold a higher order of

---

[10] Coleridge—Religious Musings.

divine manifestation, cultivated new views of life, new feelings, new aims and aspirations; aroused in him what we call the religious and moral consciousness. From the moment the law of unselfishness was recognized as divine, man sinned, wronged God and his law, every time he yielded to the temptations of the old unmoral nature. He knows that self is no longer his guide or authority; but God. Selfish interests no longer his aim; but the right. Yet none the less do all the feelings and instincts, the organic habits, of his carnal nature still throb and glow and struggle within him, ever tempting him to disobey the moral law, to live for self and not for God.

Who has not often marvelled at this strange and dire conflict that is ever going on within him? Theology has never vouchsafed a clear explanation whence this might be. The doctrine of original sinfulness has ever been a dark and mysterious one. If Evolution has not absolutely solved it, it has at least not increased the difficulty, nor contradicted any known facts in the case, but rather given a view of it that, in my estimation at least, accords more nearly with the Christian doctrine as found in the Bible than any other, goes farther toward making it comprehensible, and arouses no new difficulties, as too many other theories do, with reference to man's individual responsibility, and God's power, wisdom, and beneficence.

Finally, in the practical application of the doctrine, Evolution adds not a little force and power to it. Recognizing that sin is a relic of our low and bestial ancestors, the sinner can at least no longer pride himself on superiority over his virtuous neighbor. It is no little advantage in dealing with the former to be able to point to the verdict of science as well as the Bible, and show him that sin is invariably a sign of degradation, of reversal to a former lower type of being and inferior grade of humanity; to prove thus doubly to him that the highest manhood is the most virtuous. Character is the sole standard of judgment. The brawny prize-fighter, strong as an ox, is less of a man than the weakest child that cherishes mercy, tenderness, and pity in its heart, the mightiest conqueror, sacrificing the lives of thousands of his fellow men to his ambition, is far less heroic and great than the poorest woman who at the wash-tub sacrifices her own comfort, health, and life itself for the sustenance and happiness of her family. This is no longer mere "pious sentimentality." It is the sober verdict of pure science itself. Christ said, and Evolution fully explains and corroborates it, that "whosoever will be great among you, let him be your minister; and whosoever will be chief among you, let him be your servant." To live for others is the highest manhood. To live only for self is sinful and animal.

7

And do not the Bible and Evolution unite
their voices into one also in pronouncing Wo!
upon every one that yields to sin, and thus
helps to retard that perfect "equilibrium between constitution and conditions of existence,
which is at once the moral ideal and the limit
towards which we are progressing?" [11] Sin is not
a violation only of one set of divine laws, distinct and separate from all others. The moral
and the physical laws have one Source, and at
bottom themselves are one. Violate the moral
law, and you offend against the whole system
that governs the universe. With the same
inexorable certainty with which the penalty
follows the transgression of the physical laws
of that system, of devastating floods for denud-
ing the mountains of their timber, of sickness
for breaking the laws of health, of pain for
holding your hand in the fire,—so inevitably
must it follow every breach of the moral, or
any other, law in that system. For all are in-
extricably connected. All are interdependent
and interacting portions of one body.

And not only in the life to come will every
sin be punished; but here in this life as well.
"It is useless projecting consequences into the
future when the effects may be measured now,"
says the eminent Christian scientist, Prof.
Drummond; and then only too truly adds,

---

[11] The Study of Sociology. Cf. The Data of Ethics, vol. i.

"We are always practicing these little decep-
tions upon ourselves, postponing the consequences of our misdeeds as if they were to cul-
minate some other day about the time of death.
It makes us sin with a lighter hand to run an
account with retribution, as it were, and delay
the reckoning time with God." But "the
powers of sin, to the exact strength that we
have developed them, nearing their dreadful
culmination with every breath we draw, are
here within us, now. The souls of some men
are already honeycombed through and through
with the eternal consequences of neglect, so
that taking the natural and rational view of
their case *just now*, it is simply inconceivable
that there is any escape *just now*. What a
fearful thing it is to fall into the hands of the
living God! A fearful thing even if, as the
philosopher tells us, 'the hands of the Living
God are the Laws of Nature.'" [12]

Every sin, moreover, retards the advance of
the race by so much, retards the sinner's own
growth toward perfection and happiness, and
in some form or other brings unhappiness and
suffering upon him, and upon others. Aye, upon
others! This is the worst of all. Like the
sheen from the armor of Spenser's young Knight
of the Red Cross, so the light shed by Evolution on the foul monster of sin reveals how

---

[12] Natural Law in the Spiritual World.

" Of her there bred
A thousand young ones, which she daily fed,
Sucking from her poisonous dugs; each one
Of sundry shapes, yet all ill-favored."

For, every sin committed brings forth a whole brood of other sins in the generations to come. Every sin committed deepens the sinfulness of the character, and increases by so much the predisposition to sin, and to its attendant misery and degradation, that will be inherited by the sinner's children. If not for your own sake then, O drunkard, O libertine, O deceiver, cries Evolution, at least for the sake of your offspring yet unborn, repent, turn from the evil of your ways, and seek purity and goodness, seek God!

Yet in many other ways might it be shown how mightily Evolution strengthens and enhances the force and credibility of the practical teachings of Christianity. But it is not necessary to do this here. Enough has surely been said to show that on this doctrine as clearly as upon the others we have examined, Christianity and Evolution are not foes, but workers together toward the same end, capable of being, and, I cannot but believe, meant to be, inseparable friends and close allies, one supplementing the other in its teaching and sharpening its weapons, each strengthening the other's arm in their work, both together battling, side by side, for the same Right, Truth, and Goodness, under one and the same Captain and Lord of All.

VII.

SALVATION.

"Verily, verily, I say unto thee, Except a man be born again, he cannot see the kingdom of God."

(JOHN 3: 3.)

"By grace are ye saved through faith; and that not of yourselves; it is the gift of God."

(EPH. 2: 8.)

"That as sin hath reigned unto death, even so might grace reign, through righteousness, unto eternal life, by Jesus Christ our Lord."

(ROM. 5: 21).

> "Wenn starke Geisteskraft
> Die Elemente
> An sich herangerafft,
> Kein Engel trennte
> Geeinte Zwienatur
> Der innigen Beiden.
> Die ewige Liebe nur
> Vermag's zu scheiden."

(GOETHE—*Faust.*)

"The meaning of the sacrifice of the Cross is that self-devoting love, the surrender of the will to truth and to God, is the one thing acceptable to the Father, the one thing by which God and man are brought into harmony."

(W. H. FREMANTLE—*The Gospel of the Secular Life.*)

"We must be born again, not merely because we are wicked, not because of a lapse, but because we are flesh, and need to be carried forward and lifted up into the realm of the spirit,—a constructive rather than a reconstructive process."

(T. T. MUNGER—*The Freedom of Faith.*)

VII.

SALVATION.

IF in the preceding Study I have succeeded in making clear the teaching of Evolution on the subject of human sinfulness, then it will have appeared, not only that the scriptural doctrine is corroborated and explained thereby, but also that, from the additional light thrown on the causes and nature of sin, Evolution gives additional force and intensity to the soul's cry, "O wretched man that I am! who shall deliver me from the body of this death?" a deeper sense of the need of an answer; and also some indication at least of the directon in which the only sufficient answer must be sought. More than this we have no right to expect from a system of philosophy based wholly on scientific facts and observed phenomena. If there is nothing in these facts, and the principles legitimately based upon them, to contradict or make improbable the Christian doctrine of salvation, we ought to be satisfied; and more than satisfied if they prove to be such as to require for their natural and logical complement, such a doctrine as the Scriptures give us. For it has been asserted over and over again, with the utmost confidence and positiveness, that whatever else may be said in favor of Evolution from the Christian standpoint, the subject of salvation is one upon which they are inevitably and hopelessly antagonistic. There is no room, it is said, in the system of Evolution for any such theory of redemption and atonement as the Bible teaches. It is contrary to the whole idea of Evolution. There is not even any need of it if the principles of this philosophy be correct. Let us see.

The tendency to sin which observation and experience, as well as the Bible, tell us is inherent in man and universally prevalent, Evolution explains to be according to a well-known principle called the law of Reversion to Type. Acting through the forces of heredity, it makes itself mightily felt throughout the whole realm of organic existence; and has been a prominent agent in modifying the development of living things. Owing its existence to the forces that make for progress and improvement, it becomes itself the chief opponent of such progress, the great retarding element that hinders all improvement. In its practical workings it is a principle with which all are acquainted. Every gardener knows how, no sooner than he has succeeded in bringing forth a new and improved variety of the rose, for example, the inclination at once manifests itself to degenerate.

Let me call as witness to this fact the editor of a religious journal who does not believe in

Evolution, and whose words are quoted by a brother editor with much satisfaction as describing "facts whose truthfulness is much more patent than is that of any of the evolutionary theories,"—so little is Evolution understood!— Says this writer: "Even when the plants in a neglected garden are not altogether supplanted and dispossessed, an ominous process of degeneration sets in. The flowers, once tended with so much care, and grown to such perfection, revert to an earlier and inferior type; they lose form, color, perfume; the large 'voluptuous garden-roses,' with their infinite variety and infinite wealth of hue, sink back into the primitive dog-rose of our hedges, and the whole race of choice cultivated geraniums into the crane's-bill of the copse and the wayside. And this law of degeneration from neglect runs and holds in every province of life." Every bird-fancier has observed the same. Suppose he has a number of pigeons of all varieties of form and color. He leaves them to themselves. Not many generations need pass before each one of the varieties will have degenerated. Their different fancy colors will have given place to a sameness of a sober hue. Their distinctive forms will have vanished in great degree, and all resemble one another. In a word, give them time enough and simply leave them alone, and all the different varieties will revert to the original type of the common rock-pigeon. And this same tendency runs through all the organic world. Even in the highest and most complex forms of being, in man himself, it is often strikingly displayed. Shipwrecked sailors have been found on desert islands who in a few decades, removed from the restraining and elevating influences of society, had sunken into an almost savage state. And even in the most enlightened state, surrounded by all that refines and uplifts man, who has not often been conscious of the mighty downward-drawing tendency in his own breast; the chafing against the usages, requirements, restraints of society, of religion, of civilization itself; the impulse for once to throw them all off, to flee into the woods, to the mountains, to enjoy at least a few days or weeks of freedom, of wildness, aye, of savagery!

So universal and strong is this principle of reversion everywhere that we may well ask how, in spite of it, the world can ever have been brought to its present estate. The answer is, only by the continuous counteraction of still stronger forces. The fact is, all progress is simply the result of the battle between the hereditary forces obeying the law of reversion, and the restraining, suppressing, out-drawing and up-forcing power of an environment so wisely and beneficently ordered and controlled by the absolute Being, by divine Providence, as to improve the world, as it were in spite of itself.

Confining ourselves to man, Evolution clearly shows, just what the Bible has ever taught, that man, alone and left to himself, is lost, and that not only spiritually but physically as well. Within himself there was nothing that would have improved him; but everything that would have degraded him to the lowest possible type of being. The source of salvation must come from without. And it did. Not only from Scripture but from Evolution too, we know that the Saviour-Power was "in the beginning" active, potent in his saving work. First, as we have seen, by the necessities of primitive, half-human man's surroundings, through the struggle for existence, by the survival of the fittest, developing in him one by one his superior faculties of body and mind, and preserving and improving them by continual exercise, by inheritance, and all other beneficent means, he was lifted up above the other animals, and prepared for still higher development. Then by the necessities of his environment again he was forced into social relations with his fellowmen. These relations obliged him to conform to quite a new and different course of conduct and mode of life than that of the lower animals. Reacting upon his spiritual powers this formed new modes and habits of thought and feeling, strengthened, corrected, purified his mind; and finally, gave him the moral faculty, his conscience.

All the while that thus man was forced from without to advance and improve, from without also, by the requirements of his surroundings, he was preserved from reverting to his original condition. And then, by the reflex influence of all this, his inner condition was changed, and more and more conformed to the outer, so that in turn it acted upon the latter in the course of time. Then by the continuous beneficent agency of the Saviour, man was gradually led out and up from his low, purely animal life; and finally brought to be a moral and religious agent. That in those rude days of barbarous ignorance, though "he was in the world, the world knew him not," does not surprise us. "Such ignorance God winked at." But that now, after the lapse of ages, when man boasts of his great enlightenment and moral discernment, there should be so many who can look back over those ages and yet refuse to see the saving providence of God in it all, is indeed past comprehension.

The very same means, to bring about the same end toward which all things tended from the farthest ages of the dark past, are shown us to have been employed when we come to historic times. All through the Old Testament records we behold the same struggle between sin and God, between the natural law of reversion and the law of progress; the former steadily overcome by the enforcement of the latter through the exigencies of the environment.

What is the history of Israel but the history of human salvation, a continuation of the unwritten records of prehistoric centuries? In more detail than the latter it shows us how marvellously God was developing the spiritual nature of man, and fitting it for the consummation of his saving work. And always by the same general method. Ever we are shown how mighty was the tendency to revert still working in the Hebrew nature; now causing Israel to murmur and wish themselves back in Egypt from the threatening waters of the Red Sea; now breaking out in open rebellion against the righteous laws that governed them; then making themselves their idol calf of gold before which to bow rather than before the unseen Jehovah; lusting for the flesh-pots of their old life; and finally, even in the Holy Land degenerating by thousands and for decades of years into Baal and Astarte worship in groves and on the hill-tops. And as persistently did God drive them up and spur them on, by thunderings and hunger and wars and pestilence, by promises, warnings, gifts and allurements, appealing to sense and to soul, to yield themselves to the higher law of righteousness. Until at length, through centuries and centuries of rigorous training under the rod of the schoolmaster of outward Law, they were made ready, by its reflex influence on the inner man, for the reception of that highest type of manhood which was to be the consummation and completion of all previous training, experience, and history.

The process by which this was done was the same as that followed in the evolution of everything else. Change in the environment necessitates a ·change in the organism. For the essential condition of all life is a certain degree of correspondence between internal and external relations, even if "the continuous adjustment of internal relations to external relations" is not life itself, as Mr. Spencer maintains. Now by being obliged by Providence, manifesting itself in the environment, to conform to the law of righteousness, through centuries of time, the mental and spiritual constitution of man was gradually more and more modified, and brought into correspondence with this law, by such forces as habit, association, heredity and others. At first primitive man discerned only a very few relations as moral, saw the right and wrong, good and evil, only in a few of their most evident forms. But by being made to conform to these, his moral faculties were strengthened. By use the inner function was enlarged. This enabled him then, nay, obliged him, to recognize other and less simple ethical relations, and to live up to them. By modifying his conduct thus, his conduct in turn again exerted its reflex influence on the function, the conscience, making it still more keen-sighted, sensitive, and correct. And so on, the outer acting on the inner, and the inner on the outer, and at each step the one improving the other, the development went on. It was a slow but positive growth of the soul, a continual defeat and weakening of the tendency to reversion, a putting off the old man, and training for the final putting on of the new man. It was a steady enlargement and strengthening of the soul's capacity for God.

In all this does Evolution not simply corroborate Scripture, sometimes, it may be, in different language and terms, but yet always expressing precisely the same facts? If one is accused of having no room nor any need for the doctrine of the atonement, then how can the other escape the same charge? If one by a natural, inherent, and logical necessity almost requires us to look for a completion of the process and the coming of a perfect Man upon earth, then why not the other as well? No less clearly and positively than the Hebrew prophets does Evolution predict the time when

> " No more shall nation against nation rise,
> Nor ardent warriors meet with hateful eyes,
> Nor fields with gleaming steel be covered o'er,
> The brazen trumpet kindle rage no more,
> But useless lances into scythes shall bend,
> And the broad falchion in a plow share end;"

—when virtue, peace and righteousness shall

cover the earth as the waters cover the sea; when all men, as absolutely moral, will conform to the divine laws, as Mr. Spencer says, "not by external coercion nor self-coercion, but by acting them out spontaneously." He who has begun the good work will also finish it.

But how?

Evolution shows us how through the mutual interaction of outer and inner relations, of organism and environment, existence is brought from one stage up to the next. So plant-life is developed up to a certain point. Then animal-life is refined and ennobled up to a point where human begins. Finally human life is lifted up and up to the stage we have reached in our investigation.

Now how was plant-life graduated into animal? The final step we do not as yet know. But as every prior step was brought to pass by some new contingency in the environment necessitating some change of function, and this finally resulting in the new power, or form of life, needed for the proper correspondence between the plant and its surroundings, we are warranted in concluding that the change from mere plant to animal must have been likewise caused, after vegetal life had been far enough advanced to be capable of it, by the calling into being of the new and higher animal powers by something new in the environment, that is, not in the plant, occasioning, necessitating, the more

complex inner relations and forms of life corres
ponding to it. These again, by ever new changes
in the surroundings were developed step by step
into still higher. When animal-life was ready
at last for human faculties, they in like manner
came into being, were bestowed, in accord with
the demands of something in the environment.
If man, therefore, is to enter upon a yet higher
and different stage of being, must we not look
for it again to come through an influence from
outside of him? If the different changes in environment had not taken place, plants would
always have remained plants, animal-life would
never have attained to human. This much is
certain. And more. If it had not been for his
environment, spiritual and physical, man would
, inevitably have degenerated into a beast. If
now there come not something from without to
cause new and higher powers in man to come
into being, he will, he can, never of himself
rise above the estate in which he finds himself;
but he will and must sink down again through
the gravitation of reversion to a lower.

Is there anything in this that opposes the
Bible and Christian theology? Is there anything that they do not emphatically indorse?
Evolution does have room for, and does recognize the need of a Saviour *ab extra*. It cannot
pretend to explain the development of mankind
without recognizing the Christ as an essential
factor in it. And, as we have seen, it recog-

nizes him from the very beginning as the saving Agent in the world, and his historical appearance in the flesh as but the consummation of his eternal work of divine beneficence. So far then Evolution and the Scriptures both teach substantially the same truth. Let us question them further.

Nineteen hundred years ago the most advanced man had reached a point in his spiritual development where he could get no higher. That is to say, ethically he had learned the lesson of right and truth, he knew good from evil, and also felt that he ought to do the former and avoid the latter; and religiously he acknowledged a God who was the Maker and Ruler of all. With Æschylus he knew that

> " Jove tempers all, steadies all things that reel;
>   When wildly swerveth
> From the safe line life's burning chariot wheel
>   His hand preserveth;"

a God who demanded righteousness and condemned sin. Men had been taught that "obedience is better than sacrifice," and to ask "What profiteth the graven image, that the maker thereof hath graven it; the molten image, and a teacher of lies, that the maker of his work trusteth therein, to make dumb idols?" Man knew

> " That impious deeds conspire
> To beget an offspring of impious deeds
>   Too like their ugly sire.

> But whoso is just, though his wealth like a river
> Flow down, shall be scathless; his house shall rejoice
> In an offering of beauty forever."

With the Hebrew he believes that "the sinner shall surely die;" and with Pindar

> "No less he knows
> The day fast comes when all men must depart,
> And pay for present pride in future woes."

He even felt that he ought to love God, and that only so could he render him acceptable service.

So far had man come in the century before the present era. But he could come no farther. There was nothing in his environment to lead him beyond this. And therefore, too, we find that he was already yielding to the law of reversion. Man had begun to degenerate; or at least there were signs enough to show that he was on the point of starting on his downward and backward course. To this the later prophets bear abundant witness. The burden of their speech was that "Israel hath forgotten his Maker;" "now they sin more and more, and have made them molten images of their silver, and idols according to their own understanding. . . . O Israel, thou hast destroyed thyself." And in other civilized nations which had attained to the apex of their possible growth under their circumstances, history tells us the same story. Reversion, degeneracy, had set in. And they knew it. Unless there should speedily arise some saving circumstance, some new agency in their environment, to arrest their downward tendency, in other words, to save them from their sins, they were inevitably lost. They knew it; and eagerly they scanned the dark horizon if haply through its black and threatening clouds they might discern some rays of the star of hope. In Greece, says the late Dr. Cocker in his able work on "Christianity and Greek Philosophy," " A dim consciousness of sin and retribution as a fact, and of reconciliation as a *want*, seems to have revealed itself even in the darkest periods of history. This consciousness underlies not a few of the Greek tragedies. 'The Prometheus Bound was followed by the Prometheus Unbound, reconciled and restored through the intervention of Jove's son. The Œdipus Tyrannus of Sophocles was completed by the Œdipus Colonus, where he dies in peace amid tokens of divine favor. And so the Agamemnon and Choephoroe reach their consummation only in the Eumenides, where the Erinyes themselves are appeased and the Furies become the gracious ones.'" Among the philosophers "Plato was, in some way, able to discover the need of a Saviour, to desire a Saviour, but he could not predict his appearing. Hints are obscurely given of a Conqueror of sin, an Assuager of pain, an Averter of evil in this life, and of the impending retributions of the future life; but

they are exceedingly indefinite and shadowy.
In all instances they are rather the language of
desire, than of hope." And the same may be
said of the old Norse prophecies in the Elder
Edda, of the final regeneration, when

> "comes the mighty One
> To the great judgment;
> From heaven he comes,
> He who guides all things:
> Judgments he utters;
> Strifes he appeases,
> Laws he ordains
> To flourish forever."

Far more definitely did a Zechariah with
eager longing tell of "the Branch" who "shall
build the temple of the Lord," and call upon
Jerusalem to rejoice, for "Behold, thy King
cometh unto thee; he is just, and having salvation;" and a Malachi promise that soon
"shall the Sun of righteousness arise with healing in his wings." The spirit of man was
mellow and receptive. It needed but to come
in contact with the right agency and it would
spring into new relations and exhibit new powers. The fullness of time was come. All things
were ready and waiting.

The further truth, therefore, upon which
Christian doctrine and Evolution unite is that
the world was lost in trespasses and sin; that
it could not save itself; it needed a Saviour
from outside of itself; and one who should cause

it to undergo some radical change in its nature: it "must be born again."

˙At this stage then, says history, "when the fullness of time was come, God sent forth his Son, made of a woman, made under the law, to redeem them that were under the law, that we might receive the adoption of sons." "In him was all the fullness of the Godhead bodily." He "dwelt among us, and we beheld his glory, the glory as of the only begotten of the Father, full of grace and truth." That is, there appeared in our environment a Being essentially different from any that had ever been known; for though he "took on himself the form of a servant," and "was tempted in all points like as we are," he yet was "without sin." He was a Perfect Man, having all the positive qualities of manhood, the alone essential ones, with the essential quality of Godhood added, holiness, love. This made him the Son of God, united him with the divine by the closest bonds of real kinship; for a son is a son only as he partakes of the father's essential nature. Here, then, was a Seed of a woman who daily bruised the serpent's head; who was superior to sin and its downward tendency; who lived a higher life, the eternal, divine life. These are simply historical facts; and so are the further ones, that this Holy One and Just, after living such a perfect life, allowed himself in the very prime of his early manhood, to be arrested, mockingly tried, and unjustly, basely executed upon the cross on Calvary.

So far there seems to be no difficulty in tracing the unity of the truth as taught in Christianity and by Evolution. Nor need there be any when we come further to explain how Jesus Christ, this new Phenomenon in human environment, by his life and death became the Saviour of men, in spite of the fact that many evolutionists and many theologians strenuously deny even its possibility. The former do so on the assumption that their misrepresentation of the doctrine of the atonement is the true scriptural teaching; and the latter by accepting this misrepresentation as true and correct, and then trying to defend a theory of salvation which may have been held by some theologians, and is still too often preached even in its crudest form, but which certainly is not scriptural, rational, nor moral, and is being rapidly abandoned by the most intelligent and spiritually-minded thinkers everywhere.

The precious truth there is in the old Anselmic view of the atonement, and in Luther's and Edwards's, is freely granted. But it is no longer maintained that these contained all the truth. There was also a measure of truth in Schleiermacher's view, in Robertson's, and even in Bushnell's. None of these alone had the whole truth. Each had a part. All together have more than any one alone. The entire trend of thought to-day is to get away from the insufficiency of each, and to unite on the combined partial truths of all as one sufficient whole. "There are two tendencies," says Dr. Fisher, than whom there is none more competent to know, "which the profoundest modern theology in connection with this subject plainly discloses. The one is an unwillingness to rest in the idea of bare suffering, apart from its particular motives and concomitants, as if that alone had an atoning virtue. It is felt that suffering needlessly incurred, or arbitrarily imposed, or not growing naturally out of the providential situation in which the Sufferer is placed, would not answer the end. . . . Associated with the tendency just mentioned is the disposition to make no point of the *quantum* of suffering, as if a mathematical equivalent were to be sought for the penalty due to sin. The juridical conception of this subject, certainly in this mechanical form, is obsolescent." [1]

So long as this obsolescent concepton is still presented as the only true conception; so long as God is still spoken of substantially as Calvin represented him, holding that "in a wonderful and divine manner, He both hated us and loved us at the same time," and man is still declared, even in the very words of Edwards, to be sustaining the relation of client to Christ his Pa-

---

[1] Grounds of Theistic and Christian Belief.

tron over against God whom he has offended,
and to whom he is reconciled, strictly in the
manner of an ordinary law-suit, through the
mediation of the Patron by virtue of God's being the Friend of the latter;—so long as the
grain of truth in these conceptions is thus disguised under a mass of crudities of statement
and distorted imagery, it is no great wonder
that it gives offence not only to evolutionists,
but to not a few other thinking people as well.

At the same time I can well understand why
such and other kindred views of Christ's salvation should so long have maintained their hold
on the human mind. They satisfy a certain
natural feeling of revenge that too often is
mistaken for "righteous anger" and a just desire
for punishment. Even so careful and profound
a theologian as Canon Mozley, I cannot but
think, has fallen into this error when he says
that "it is undoubtedly the case, however we
may account for it, that the real suffering of
another for him, of a good person for a guilty
one, will mollify the appetite for punishment,
which was possibly up to that time in full
possession of our minds; and this kind of satisfaction to justice, and appeasing of it, is involved in the Scriptural doctrine of the Atonement." Surely the "appetite for punishment"
that is appeased by "this kind of satisfaction,"
is not a sense of justice, but solely and alone
an instinctive desire for revenge.

Then, too, it is agreeable to other tendencies of our carnal nature simply to accept personal safety as a ready-made gift, no matter how it was procured for us. This Robertson forcibly points out in his fine sermon on "Caiaphas' View of Vicarious Atonement." "There is a kind of acquiescence in the Atonement which is purely selfish. The more bloody the representation of the character of God, the greater, of course, the satisfaction in feeling sheltered from it. The more Wrath instead of Love is believed to be the Divine name, the more may a man find joy in believing that he is safe. It is the Siberian feeling: the innocent has glutted the wolves, and we may pursue our journey in safety. Christ has suffered, and I am safe. He bore the agony—I take the reward. I may live now with impunity, and, of course, it is very easy to call acquiescence in that arrangement humility, and to take credit for the abnegation of self-righteousness."

But it is not to our purpose to dwell upon such erroneous theories. None of them, surely, are necessarily implied in the Scriptural account of the saving work of the God-Man. As surely much of them is contrary to the conceptions of the divine nature, the nature of man and of sin, and the spirit of Christ's life and teachings, as given in the Bible and in human consciousness. As such, therefore, they cannot contain the essential truth on which alone Evolution

could unite with them. Phases of it, indeed,
they may express. Propitiation, Satisfaction,
Expiation, Reconciliation, Sacrifice, Substitution, all such words are expressive of ideas that
enter into the explanation of the method of
salvation. But all of them, too, are liable to
misuse, and capable of conveying wholly wrong
ideas. The truth in them cannot be literally
translated. It must be spiritually apprehended.

How, then, according to the Scriptures and
according to Evolution did the appearance of
Jesus Christ, his work upon earth, and death
on the cross, effect the regeneration of man?

That it did so, is still doing so, we know.
But we want the fact explained. It was not
by reversing the great law of degeneracy,
through divine interference; nor by abrogating
or changing any other physical or moral law
of the universe. Such a thing is simply unthinkable. And we have his own assurance
that he came not to destroy, but to fulfill, to
complete. Neither was it only or mainly to
tell men what they must do, how they must
live, in order to be saved. This they knew
before. That without holiness no man can
come to God was a truth that not only their
prophets, but their own bitter experience,
had been ever more and more painfully im-
pressing upon them. The one thing man now
needed was a new motive-power within his
breast, stronger than any other he had, dif-

ferent from any other, a God-ward working power that would counteract and overcome the deathward forces striving within him. To kindle this in the human heart, and so destroy sin, Christ came; to implant the principle of a higher order of existence; to "bring life and immortality to light."

Does any one ask what that new power was? Inquire of your own hearts. What was the saving principle that rescued you from sin and from death, that impelled you to shrink from evil with an agony of horror, and to live a new life full of zeal for the good and the true, a life in God? What is it that keeps you hourly from yielding to temptation, comforts and strengthens you in seasons of sorrow and pain, preserves a mighty peace deep down in your innermost soul, even while the storms of trouble and anguish are raging on the surface without? Love. Aye, there is only one power in heaven or on earth that can counteract the terrible influence of hereditary tendencies to sin and evil; only one power that abideth and continues perseveringly in well-doing; only one power that can change the character and life from self-seeking and self-indulgence to self-forgetful, self-sacrificing devotion to the Divine. And that power is Love, the power that made the world, that sustains it ever, and that will lift it into heaven in the end. That power is the Spirit of God himself; for "God is love."

Love to God! Such a thing was unknown among men before Christ came. He first brought it down from heaven to earth. Hitherto men had known God only to dread him, or to admire, often to hate and scorn him in their secret hearts. He had been to them nothing but some far-off majesty, whose hard decrees had to be obeyed; who gave blessings to the obedient, and was terrible in his punishment of the disobedient. Even the Hebrew, who had the loftiest conceptions of God to be found in any people of his time, even he regarded him only as an almighty Creator, all-wise Ruler; as an unseen individual Monarch, worthy to be adored, and to whom gratitude and praise belonged for all his mercies. But he could not love him in any true sense. He was too awful in the splendor and glory of his holiness; and he was too far-off; though none could ever escape from his presence, yet was there ever an infinite, abysmal gap between him and his most saintly worshipper. Within the inner veil of the Holy of Holies no one might ever go save the high-priest only, and he but once a year. To see God was to die. To touch even the outside of the holy Ark whereon was his Mercy-Seat was to share the instant fate of the blasphemer. How could sinful man dare to love such a Being, even had he felt the impulse to do so? He knew that he ought to; but he neither felt the glow of love in his heart, nor knew how to apply and direct it if it had been there.

What was needed, therefore, first and foremost, was a manifestation of the Divine such as should cause an adaptation and adjustment of the inner relations in man to God different from those hitherto existing. Such a manifestation Christ is. In him is God manifest in the flesh. The Expression of the divine Essence, the Word, that had been in the beginning with God, that was God, that had been in the world and by whom the world was made, yet never had been recognized by men while in his abstract form, now was concentrated into a concrete, visible shape; the Word was made flesh and dwelt among us, so that we beheld his excellence and recognized it as the excellence, the very essence, of the Divinity. Men saw it to be not only, or even chiefly, physical power, but pre-eminently grace and truth, purity, tenderness, sympathy, sweetness, love. In these the almighty Power consisted. Not to command and compel; but to draw all men unto him. Not to destroy by physical strength; but to overcome evil with good.

It was a new revelation of God, such as had never been dreamed of by man. He had indeed been taught in abstract words of the righteousness, the holiness, and even the fatherly love of the Deity. But his narrow, carnal mind had not been able to grasp the full meaning of the

broad, spiritual fact. He had never understood
what are the contents of the divine entirety.
He needed to learn from parts to whole, the
pure white blaze of the eternal Light only
dazzled and blinded him. He needed to have
its rays separated into their component colors.
And this Christ did by the prism of his human
personality. Now he shone upon the troubled
and perplexed family at Cana with the beams
of a delicate, sympathetic considerateness, by
supplying the wine that was needed for the due
observance of their glad marriage festival. God
had often before given them wine. Every
season they gathered the rich clusters full of
purple juice. But never before had it struck
them as now that it was the gift of a gentle
care and interest in their happiness. And surely
never after would they enjoy the juice of the
grape without a glow of gratitude in their hearts
for the divine love that employed omnipotence
itself in ministering to their comfort and needs.
They saw God in a new aspect. Henceforth
he was more to them, and other, than the
Jehovah of whom they had heard and read in
the synagogue. They had new feelings, they
acted differently, toward him than before. At
Sychar by the ancient well he shone with the
rays of sweet pity and irresistibly pure love
upon the heart of the abandoned, profligate
adulteress. She who so long had defied the
God whom men taught, was in a moment

melted to trustful confidence, confession of her sins, deep penitence, and enthusiastic love. The exposure of her evil did not make her defiant. But so gently, so pityingly was it done that her inmost soul was touched. Contrition filled her breast. The beauty and strength of purity were revealed to her, and her whole being sank in adoration down before it. She had never known God before. Now she knew him. "I that speak to thee am he!" Was this God? This the love of God? Could purity be so gentle, pity so sweet, righteousness so helpful, uplifting? To meet God had been a terrifying, unendurable thought. She met him; he was Love itself. To part from him now was pain. He was a Spirit, a Principle of life; forever would she stay with him, move and have her being in him.

So in scores and hundreds of cases the God-Man manifested forth his excellence. Now touching sight into eyes born blind, now speaking speech into tongues that were dumb; then looking strength into palsied limbs, health into the sick, wholeness to the lame and halt; and again feeding the hungry by thousands, weeping with the tearful that stood by their new-made graves, or speaking life into bodies dead for days. Wherever there was want, he relieved it; where there were sorrow and grief, he assuaged them; where there were fallen ones, or falling, he lifted them up. Wherever

help was needed for body or soul, he was the
Helper; where darkness was, he the Light;
where sin and death were, he was the Resurrection and the Life. Everywhere he was the
same Love, shedding forth his saving rays like
the sun, in a myriad different hues and directions, that men might know of what the perfect
white Light consists, what God is.

And how black and ugly in this light appeared the shadows of sin! Before, sin had
been known only as a transgression of the
Commandments; now it was seen to be far
more than this, an ingrate spurning of a Friend's
true and faithful love; no more only wrong
conduct, but the mark of a bad character, a
mean, low, corrupt heart. And souls, moreover, that had scarcely suspected its presence
before, suddenly became conscious thereof,
smote themselves on the breast, and cried out
with broken and contrite hearts, "God be mer-
ciful to me a sinner!" Priests, Scribes, Pharisees, Sadducees, the rich and noble, the honored
and respected, who 'neath their fine exterior
had kept their inner vileness hidden from their
fellows, were now seen by all as they were.
Their rigid legalism and punctilious ritualism
no longer sheltered them. Ah, how they
writhed under the exposure! How they hated
him who had torn off their masks! Straightway the oneness of Sin appeared. It is all the
brood of one monster principle. And now that

8

danger threatened, behold how it instinctively revealed its kinship! Secret and open sinners, Pharisee and Sadducee, Jew and Roman, rich and poor, low and high, all who before had hated one another, now suddenly were drawn together into an intimate fellowship and close alliance, to entrap, to betray, to destroy this Holy One. As never before men saw the fundamental unity of all sin in however many and varied forms it might appear; and its all-pervading presence no less, its terrible strength and power. No wonder the race had been degenerating with such a deadly force at work within it!

And how should ever the divine Life-principle supplant this deeply rooted Death-principle in human nature? How would ever love to God be made to take the place of hatred to God, which sin essentially is? In order to this it was necessary for men clearly to distinguish between the divine in Christ and his mere human personality. They would have to love not only the lovely man, but the Love in the man; and not only this, but also the Love distinct from the man, wherever and in whatever form it might manifest itself. From loving and following the gentle, pure, honest, forgiving, self-sacrificing Nazarene, they needed to love and follow gentleness, purity, honesty, self-sacrifice themselves, as divine, living principles, rays of the pure Spirit of God. This

Christ told his disciples over and over again, assuring them "It is expedient for you that I go away: for if I go not away, the Comforter will not come unto you," "even the Spirit of truth; whom the world cannot receive, because it seeth him not, neither knoweth him: but ye know him; for he dwelleth with you, and shall be in you."

Nothing is clearer than that Christ realized this necessity more and more the more he felt the growing affection and devotion of his followers. His anxiety to keep plainly before them the distinction between his human personality and his essential divine self often becomes painfully evident. He dwells upon it continually. "He that believeth on me," he says, "believeth not on me, but on him that sent me. And he that seeth me seeth him that sent me." He whom they beheld was only the manifestation in the flesh of the Eternal One who is a Spirit. For the same reason he so often speaks of himself in terms incompatible with his being as an individual human person: "I am the Way, and the Truth, and the Life," he says; "Before Abraham was, I am;" "Abide in me, and I in you." Even though made flesh, yet always he remained the eternal Word.

But how difficult was it to teach this fact to his followers! It must needs be that the Word be severed from the flesh if this truth should ever be fully learned.   Did he remain with men in visible form, they would inevitably confound the form with the essence, and love the Man instead of the God.   Therefore the "expediency" for them that he go away, even though it be full of the pain and disgrace of a cruel death for himself.   With infinite tenderness and delicacy did he try to prepare his loved ones for the tremendous sacrifice to be made voluntarily, out of pure love for them.   "A little while, and ye shall not see me."   And when even their affection blinded them so that they would not comprehend his sad meaning, he finally had to say plainly, "I came forth from the Father, and am come into the world: again I leave the world, and go to the Father." Now they must surely understand that their good Shepherd would lay down his life for the sheep.

Nor were they long left in doubt as to what was the wolf and the robber.   The great Adversary had all the while stealthily, cautiously, cunningly, been concentrating his wicked forces for the final blow.   The Serpent had drawn his hideous coils ever tighter around the Innocent One.   He raised his hateful crest to strike;—it was Sin.   And every sinner felt, and must still feel to-day, "In so far as I have sinned, I had a part in that crime; I helped to betray, I helped to crucify him.   He died because of my sins as much and as really as for the sins of the Scribes

and Pharisees." But Love also was ready.
It would not shirk the pain. It would face the
death which sin had enthroned in the world,
would bear the penalty, innocent yet "made
sin for us," and bearing thus the sin of the world
would conquer the world and sin. Love should
not be destroyed by death; but by dying should
forever take from death its venomous sting.
Strongly, therefore, heroically, sublimely, it
faced the foul attack. Cursed and reviled, it
blessed in return. Smitten on one cheek, it
turned the other. Never an angry word es-
caped it; not even a murmur of impatience.
Under the weight of the cross, it wept indeed,
but wept for the godless city below. Hanging
in agony upon it, it thought of the bereaved
disciple, and cared for the desolate mother.
With the spear piercing its side, it prayed
"Father, forgive them!" them who pierced
me, them whose sins killed me; all sinners, for
all had part in the crime; all men, for all have
sinned.

The victory was won. Having loved his
own, he loved them to the end. It was fin-
ished. Love had endured the final, supreme
test. The fatal power of sin had been demonstrated, and the vital power of holiness as well.
He died for us once, that we might die unto
sin. The Way of Life was opened; through
the very gates of Death it leads. To live unto
God is to die unto self and to the world. The

Man Christ was dead. But the God Christ could say, "Lo, I am with you always, even to the end of the world." Love would now abide forever upon earth; a new and mighty element in human environment, to which henceforth men must adjust themselves, or die. To live now means to bring the character into correspondence with this eternal reality. The sinner who refuses, perishes. "The wages of sin is death."

Such is an outline of the facts drawn from the sacred history, the precious facts by which the world is saved. It shows us how by the life and death of Jesus Christ a new factor was brought into human environment, requiring a new adaptation of man's life thereto, and thereby generating new and higher powers, a new and higher form of existence: life eternal. It thus accords fully with the requirements of Evolution.

On the other hand, it sustains the essential truths of Christian theology, so far as this correctly interprets the historical facts. There is, indeed, nothing in it of the heathen idea of sacrifice, of an offering made to an angry Deity to appease him, or to "satisfy," in this sense, outraged Justice. There is no literal substitution of an innocent victim, dragged by the guilty ones to the altar to suffer the punishment they deserved, and thus buying their immunity. Nor is there any such notion in it of "imputed

righteousness," and "imputed sin," as has been
held and preached by some. But it includes
under it the truer view of Mozley and that of
Robertson. The former truly says that the
scriptural doctrine of the Atonement involves
"a moral kind of substitution. It is one person
suffering in behalf of another, for the sake of
another: in that sense he takes the place and
acts in the stead of another. . . . But this
is the moral substitution which is inherent in
acts of love and labor *for* others; it is a totally
different thing from the literal substitution of
one person for another in punishment." [2] At
the same time it shows that Christ did live and
die in our stead in a true sense. As Robertson
declares, "That he died for all is true—first,
Because he was the victim of the sin of all.
. . . Again, he died for all, in that his
sacrifice represents the sacrifice of all. . . .
Gazing on that perfect Life, we, as it were,
say, 'That is my religion, that is my righteousness—what I want to be, which I am not; that
is my offering, my life as I would wish to give
it,—freely and not checked, entire and perfect.'" [3] And our view too, in so far embraces
that of Schleiermacher, that "by the sufferings
of Christ punishment may be said to be abol-
ished, because in the communion of his blessed

---

[2] University Sermons.
[3] Sermons.

life, evil, which becomes a vanishing element, is no longer felt as a penalty. It is in his sufferings that we behold his holiness, and his blessedness also, which are seen to be invincible under the severest test. By entering into his sufferings, the conviction of his holiness and blessedness is brought home to us."

No violence is thus done to the doctrine of a vicarious sacrifice; for the life and death of Christ were most truly vicarious. And only as we make Christ our real Vicar, our great and perfect Representative, do we reap any saving virtue from him. But this can only be done by ourselves so living, so conforming our being to his, that he may truly represent us.

The idea even that Christ's sacrifice *induced* God to save us, while not true in its bare literalness, may yet be said to be involved in one aspect of the case. It changed God's relation to man, by changing man's relation to God. So likewise it may be said to have *enabled* God to save man, by removing the great hinderance in man, namely sin, which stood in the way of his salvation. It was an actual removal and destruction of sin,—not indeed as an abstract, outward, objective thing, a cloud hanging between the divine and the human, but as a subjective power and agency working in man,—by constraining him through love to renounce and abolish sin in his life, and practice righteousness instead. In this sense, too, it caused divine justice to be "satisfied," since it gave to man the impulse and power to be just henceforth, making him be just, and thus really "justifying" him. "It was not the satisfaction of justice apart from love, nor as the precedent condition of the revelation of love. For in relation to the law there was not merely the satisfaction, but the fulfillment of the law. It was not a satisfaction of justice by the imposition upon the innocent of the punishments of the guilty, nor, by the substitution of an equivalent of the measure through a series of legal fictions, and in that there would be no measure of gain. In a higher sense justice is satisfied when righteousness is actualized on the earth. Justice is vindicated when it is asserted and established. It is not a compensation to balance injustice that is required, nor an equivalent for sin or for the sequences of sin, but the power to overcome evil, and to bring men out of sin." [4]

Nothing of all this would have been brought to pass if Christ had not died. By his death, therefore, he became our Justification, he purchased salvation for us, became our Redeemer, the Ransom by which we are loosed from the bonds of sin and of death.

In all this, it will be seen, there is nothing incompatible with the theory of Evolution. That theory may rather be said not only to

---

[4] Elisha Mulford—The Republic of God.

admit, but implicitly to require it. For it everywhere recognizes the great law, the universal law of love, of which the atonement is but an application and exemplification, according to which all advance from inferior to superior, from lower to higher, forms of being is ever brought about only through sacrifice and suffering. "Except a corn of wheat fall into the ground and die, it abideth alone," nothing higher comes from it; "but if it die, it bringeth forth much fruit." Except a woman endure agony and pain, and herself descend to the very borders of the grave, she may not reach the high estate of motherhood and give life to an immortal soul. Always the higher must reach down to lift up the lower. Ever the above can draw up to itself the below only by paying the price of suffering and sacrifice. It is the "expiation " that superiority makes for inferiority. It is the divine law that lifted up Christ on the cross so that he might draw all men unto him, the law of perfect love. It was dimly foreshadowed in the Hebrew ritual in which "without shedding of blood is no remission;" abundantly illustrated in nature; recognized by science; and finally fulfilled in the highest sphere when the Lamb of God was slain for us on Calvary's altar.

At the same time the law still operates and must be obeyed by every one who would reap its blessings. And any view of the atonement

that would make its efficacy consist in Christ's
having done something, or suffered something,
in order that we might not have to do it, certainly does violence to this truth, is incompatible with the principles of Evolution, and unwarranted by Scripture. These in no wise
oppose, however, but freely accept the truer
view that the practical efficacy lay in his giving
us the inclination and power to live a higher
life, a life different from the carnal life of selfishness, and based on the principle of pure,
unselfish love. While, as we have seen, we
may speak of the effect of Christ as changing
the attitude of God towards man, pleasing, re-
conciling, satisfying, propitiating him, it must
ever be borne in mind that such language cannot be taken literally, but must be spiritually
interpreted. In God is no variableness neither
shadow of turning. The only change that is
possible, and the only that is necessary in
order to man's salvation, is in our attitude to
God. No change of thought, feeling or disposition in him is required, even if it were thinkable. But a radical change in us is absolutely essential, a change of our whole nature and mode
of life, a thorough conversion, an entire regeneration. In this alone consists the saving
efficacy of the atonement. And this truth is
being clearly recognized by the profoundest
theologians, who, like Canon Mozley, admit that
"The atoning act of the Son, as an act of love on

behalf of sinful man, appealed to wonder and
praise; the effect of the act in changing the
regard of the Father towards the sinner, was
only the representation, in the sublime and ineffable region of mystery, of an effect which men
recognized in their own minds." [s]

It is not less truly, however, on this account,
an atonement that was made for man by Christ.
But it recognizes the necessity of man's share
in the work in order to a share in the fruits.
It gives a reason for the requirement of faith on
which the Scriptures so strenuously insist. As
in Christ there was an at-onement between
the divine and the human, so our salvation from
sin and the redemption of the entire race, depend upon the same at-onement which is made
possible by the removal of sin through the love
for God which Christ's life and death called into action in man, impelling man to adjust himself to the divine, to bring himself into the
same conformity with God that subsisted in
Christ; to hide his life with Christ in God.
The Saviour's work consisted in bringing the
Love-Spirit, God, into human consciousness.
Man's work, in order to be saved, consists in
adjusting his life to this Spirit. In the words
of Erskine: "The dispensation of Christ embraces in it a oneness with the mind of God;
not merely a readiness to do his will when we

---

[s] University Sermons.

know it, but a participation in his mind, so that
by a participation in the divine nature we enter
into the reason of his will, and do not merely
obey the authority of his will." [*] Thus it is true in
the highest sense that we "are saved by grace,"
or love; by this new factor brought by Christ
into man's conscious environment.

But it is equally true that while "saved by
grace," it is "through faith." Not indeed by
any magic virtue inhering in, or imputed to, the
mere act of belief. But simply through man's
accepting the new saving factor in his environment, and making Love the foundation principle of his life. This is faith, as Dr. Lyman
Abbott once defined it, I think in *The Christian
Union*, "the perception and reception of God in
and through Christ Jesus."

This is the faith that effects the new birth;
changes radically man's whole nature, converting, turning him to the higher spiritual life of
holiness, from the lower carnal life of sin in
which he was reverting to brute existence. It
puts off from him the old man with his selfish
principles and downward tendencies, and puts
on the new man who is renewed in the image
of God. It is this faith that fulfills the exhorta-
tion of Paul, "Be not conformed to this world:
but be ye transformed by the renewing of your
mind, that ye may prove what is that good, and

---

[*] Memoirs.

acceptable, and perfect, will of God;" and makes us understand the meaning of his strange assertion, "I live: yet not I, but Christ liveth in me." By this faith is the reversionary tendency in human life arrested. In the love by which faith worketh, from which it is inseparable, is the power applied by which alone this tendency can be permanently counteracted and overcome. By it is the spirit freed from the choking grasp of sin and brought into communion with the Eternal Spirit, in whom alone is Life, severance from whom is Death.

It will have been noticed that the view advanced as the one on which Evolution and the Scriptures can unite, does not lay as much stress as is commonly done on personal escape from the penalty of sin, whether in this life or in the future. It does not look upon this as a consideration of the first importance. At the same time it is clearly implied.

The penalty of sin being not an arbitrarily imposed punishment, but a natural and necessary consequence of wrong-doing, it follows of course that, as soon as the latter is stopped, the former will cease. Remove the cause, and the effect will be removed. Not, however, absolutely and wholly. We reap the penalty of sins long ago committed, and for which deep penitence may have sprung up in our breasts. So also we often have to partake in the penalty of others' sins, sins which we did not and would not commit.

These are facts of experience that remain whatever theory of atonement we may adopt. And they show the error and futility, as well as the moral wrong, of holding up escape from uncomfortable penalties as an inducement for men to forsake sin, to repent and believe. True repentance, real saving faith, must have a different motive than selfishness in any form. But it is also no less a fact of experience, I think, that from all such suffering the sting of guilt is removed. We have to endure the penalty whether we repent or not. But how differently after than before conversion! Afterwards, when we realize that it is the result of past sins, we accept it with patient humility. We feel that it is but just. Before, too, we may have felt its justice; but this only added to its pain; and how we rebelled against it! It was a thousand times harder to bear than now; the real quantum of suffering in us was a thousand times greater. And when we are called on to endure our share of the penalty of the world's sin, we do so precisely as we accept the consequence of ignorantly breaking any of the physical laws of nature. It is a part of the inexorable, beneficent order by which God directs the world. It may be physically painful. But there is no sense of individual guilt, no reproach of conscience, no feeling of self-despising, nor revelation of an ingrate, bad character. This removal of the consciousness of badness, of moral guilt, is all that we mean by pardon and forgiveness. It is all that the facts warrant. It is the result indeed of our standing in different relations to God than before; but surely not the consequence of God's having changed his attitude towards us. It is a change in our spirit; not in the eternally Unchangeable One.

What then is the conclusion of the whole matter? What are the facts on which Evolution and Christianity are at one?

Simply these: Before Christ came the world had reached a stage in its development where it was not only ready to enter upon a new and higher stage, but where, if it did not do this, it would inevitably degenerate, through the inherent tendency to reversion which manifests itself in every organism, and can be counteracted only by new adjustments between the inner and outer relations, called forth by some essential change in the environment. In other words, the world was lost in trespasses and sin. It was becoming consciously worse and worse. It could only be saved by the generation of a new power within man stronger than the inherent principle of sin. This could be produced only by some such occurrence outside of it as would bring about a change of nature within it. Then came Christ, Son of Man and Son of God at once, "to seek and to save that which was lost." By his pure and blameless life wholly for others, and his innocent death a Sacrifice for sin, he destroyed the power of sin and death, and brought the infinite love of God, a working, saving power, into human consciousness. This induces a re-adjustment of man's thoughts, feelings, powers, actions, to God, to his fellow men, to himself, and to all the world. It generates love as a permanent motive principle and rule of life in the character. It conforms man more and more to God and his laws, and then, reflexly also transforms the spiritual nature of man himself. Man is saved by love through faith, is made a new creature, with new and lofty aspirations, new capabilities and powers, becomes also a son of God. By this process he is raised higher and higher, and brought into closer and closer union with the divine. From hopeless death he is rescued and prepared for a perfect and eternal life. For "Perfect correspondence," in the words of Herbert Spencer, "would be perfect life. Were there no changes in the environment but such as the organism had adapted changes to meet, and were it never to fail in the efficiency with which it met them, there would be eternal existence and universal knowledge." ' Or as the same truth is expressed by One greater than Spencer, "This is life eternal, that they might know thee the only true God, and Jesus Christ, whom thou hast sent."

' Principles of Biology, vol. i.

VIII.

RELIGION.

"Thou shalt love the Lord thy God with all thy heart, and with all thy soul, and with all thy mind. This is the first and great commandment. And the second is like unto it, Thou shalt love thy neighbor as thyself."

(MATT. 22: 37–39.)

"How truly its central position is impregnable, religion has never adequately realized."

(HERBERT SPENCER—*First Principles.*)

"Now that Science has made the world around articulate, it speaks to Religion with a twofold purpose. In the first place it offers to corroborate Theology, and in the second to purify it."

(HENRY DRUMMOND—*Natural Law in the Spiritual World.*)

"Christianity is not primarily a system of doctrines arranged in rational order, but a system of beings in right relation to God and in harmony with each other."

(NEWMAN SMYTH, *in Andover Review.*)

"It is not a system of worship that Christianity came to bring to mankind. . . . . It came to bind men together in just and true relations, to infuse into their societies the Divine spirit, to transfigure the coarse vesture of humanity with that divinity which is love, till it shall become a temple in which He dwells."

(W. H. FREMANTLE—*The Gospel of the Secular Life.*)

"The Christian religion will be the redemption of the natural man out of his disunion from God into freedom in God through the full revelation of God's grace in Jesus Christ, the object of its faith."

(BIEDERMANN—*Christl. Dogmatik—quoted by*
Dr. S. Harris in The Self-Revelation of God.)

VIII.

RELIGION.

In concluding this series of Studies with the discussion of the subject of religion, I do not intend to treat of the history of religion, of its origin and growth. The theory of Evolution on this subject has been already incidentally given with sufficient fullness for our purpose. Recognizing with Lowell that

"God sends his teachers unto every age,
To every clime, and every race of men,
With revelations fitted for their growth
And shape of mind, nor gives the realm of Truth
Into the selfish rule of one sole race:
Therefore each form of worship that hath swayed
The life of man, and given it to grasp
The master-key of knowledge, reverence,
Infolds some germs of goodness and of right;" [1]

Evolution accepts the verdict of comparative theology with reference to the heathen religions, as expressed by one of the ablest contributors to that science, Dr. James Freeman Clarke, who says, "They must contain more truth than error, and must have been, on the whole, useful to mankind. We do not believe that they originated in human fraud, that their es-

---

[1] Rhœcus.

sence is superstition, that there is more false-
hood than truth in their doctrines, that their
moral tendency is mainly injurious."[2]   But at
the same time it fully realizes that they were
only tentative religions, and that in Christianity
we have the most fully developed flower that
the trunk of divine truth has yet brought forth.
The little grain of mustard seed sown in Pales-
tine has already become "the greatest among
herbs," the most perfect religion that has ever
appeared.   Rejoicing in this fact, yet at the
same time humbly acknowledging that its
fruits, meant for the healing of the nations and
the bringing of peace on earth and good will
towards men, are not all that could be desired,
I simply wish to examine it in the light we
have gained from the application of the principles of Evolution in the foregoing studies.   For
I believe that with the aid of this light we shall
see more clearly than otherwise why this highest form of religion is not bringing forth fruits
more commensurate with its capabilities, and
accordant with its lofty aim; and especially also
shall be made to understand what religion is
meant to do, can do, and must do for the salvation of mankind, if it would be loyal to its own
Scriptures; what we must do if we would not
be untrue to ourselves, our fellow men, and to
our God.

---

[2] Ten Great Religions.   vol. i.

The essential element in all religion is the striving after union with God. This may have been very vague and feeble in the earlier, lowest forms of religion; but it is the avowed aim and purpose of Christianity, the latest, highest form. Upon the view then that we take of the being and nature of God, and of man, will depend our view of what constitutes union between them, and of how it is to be effected; will depend, in short, the character of our religion.

The prevalent restlessness in theology, and perturbation of men's religion, are mainly caused, directly or indirectly, by the modification Evolution has made in the popular conception of God. It has shown him to be in many respects different from the representation that had become traditional. Hence there has to be a re-adjustment of all our beliefs and practices in so far as they relate to God. This is now going on in the religious world, to the alarm of many, and the harm of some, perhaps, but surely only to the permanent benefit of the true religion. Thus the divine truth has ever grown in the past. With every new and higher conception of God there has been a new co-ordination of dogmas and practices to bring them into some kind of harmony with it. "If the god be an ideal of beauty," says Baring-Gould, "and his worship be conducted on a type the perfection of ugliness, one of two results must ensue; the idea of the god will be lowered to the type of worship, or the service will be revolted from by the worshipper. Thus, some of the Mexican gods were ideally beneficent and holy, and the devotion felt towards them exhibited itself in the sacrifice of that which by man is regarded as the most precious offering he can make— human life. When these benevolent gods' altars reeked with gore, their own character deteriorated, and they came to be regarded as blood-thirsty and malicious deities. Man at once perceives the incongruity between the mode of worship and the idea of the object worshipped, and he seeks to harmonize them in the best way he can, generally by dragging the idea of God to the level of the mode of worship, rather than by elevating the worship to conform to the idea of God." [3] Whether we agree with this writer or not on this last point, the fact certainly cannot be denied that from the very nature of religion, its character must in the first place be determined, in great part at least, by the conception of God that prevails.

It is plain, therefore, that so long as the God of Heine's childhood is retained in the popular representation, a benignant old man looking down upon his terrestrial creation from some window in the far-off celestial domain; or the God of the Duke of Argyll, moved by "mental

---

[3] Origin and Development of Religious Belief, vol. i.

affections," a being "who hates evil and is angry with the wicked every day;" or a dread Lawgiver issuing his decrees from his great white throne; so long as God is thought of as a Being with all the limitations implied in human personality, in parts and attributes such as man has, only greater; so long our religion must be not only imperfect and partial, but erroneous and inconsistent to an unwarrantable extent.

I know that such wrong conceptions are not taught in the Scriptures if spiritually interpreted. I know that theology no longer teaches them. And even in the popular belief they are more and more being abandoned. But I know also with equal positiveness that just such conceptions are yet taught in more than half the pulpits of our land; that in by far the most of our Sunday-schools our children are indoctrinated with them; and that they are the ideas that still dominate the current popular religion, and make that religion so largely to consist of a mere dead formalism, or cold intellectualism, or still worse, of actually irreligious superstition.

After what has been shown to be the teaching of Evolution as to the being and nature of God, I need not here again point out how utterly opposed it is to such false notions, nor how fully in harmony with the teachings of the Scriptures and of the most advanced Chris-

tian theology. I will content myself, therefore, with showing in mere outline, its direct
bearing upon true religion, and the great
advantage the latter must derive from it.

What has aroused the fiercest attacks upon
Evolution and gained for it the name of the
philosophy of nescience, and agnosticism, is the
circumstance that Mr. Spencer declares God to
be the Great Unknown and Unknowable. But
as we saw, the principles of Evolution are not
principles of nescience; agnosticism in the common acceptation of the term is impossible upon those principles, and Mr. Spencer cannot
mean the words Unknown and Unknowable to
be taken in their absolute sense. I am glad
that this conviction has been corroborated since
I first expressed it, by an English writer whose
minute and long acquaintance with Mr.
Spencer's works and opinions must make him
an authority on the subject, and who in his able
"Examination of the Structural Principles of
Mr. Spencer's Philosophy," has given us the
fullest, fairest, and most thorough critique of
Evolution that has yet been written anywhere.
This author, the Rev. W. D. Ground, declares
on this point that "Mr. Spencer's whole assertion only means that God is uncomprehended
and incomprehensible." It could not mean
anything else. And this the Bible declares as
positively as Evolution, and theology is coming to realize more and more clearly.

Far from being a cause for reproach to Evolution, this is one of the important contributions it has made to religion. From the time that Moses inquired on Horeb into the nature of the Most High and had to be silenced by the rebukeful, majestic declaration, "I Am that I Am," the tendency has ever been strong in man first to surmise, to speculate; then to affirm and dogmatize; and to end by denouncing and cursing all who will not accept his speculative conclusions. Obeying this tendency he has almost invariably succeeded only in degrading God. The little that he knew and could know of the divine he quickly supplemented with much that he imagined; and then the chief end of his religion speedily became nothing more than, on the one hand, to worship this creature of his own making, and on the other, to defend it against those of his fellows who could or would not think and feel and fancy as he did. The real purpose of religion nearly always therefore was made altogether a secondary matter, or lost sight of altogether. Hence the otherwise strange fact, revealed by the study of religions and by the history of the Christian Church as well, that the more definite and detailed the creeds which men have held, the less vital, practical, and real their religion. Not that they knew or believed too much, but they thought they knew more than they did, and that this pseudo-knowledge was exalted even above their real knowledge, and distracted the attention from the latter itself.

The great merit of Evolution is that it strips our belief of so many cumbersome pseud-ideas. It shows clearly that all we can possibly know of the nature of the Supreme Being is very little; but that little is enough, and is so certain and plain that there can be no dispute about it. All beyond this is not positive knowledge at all, but mere inference, speculation, and supposition. It is not on that account necessarily wrong or useless. But it is unessential. And above all, it can never be more than personal opinion, which may be held or may not, without in any wise affecting a person's vital religion. Hold to the few clear, known truths of God, as alone essential; and whatever else you may believe or not believe will not affect your religiousness. No one else may condemn you therefor, neither may you condemn another. What a blessing it would be if this spirit were once to be fully adopted in the religious world.

Nor is this, as has sometimes been charged, mere indifferentism. Evolution insists as strenuously as possible that, as far as known, God is really known. With no uncertain sound it echoes the voice of the great I Am. The God who is a Spirit is a fact "deeper than demonstration, deeper even than definite cogni-

tion, deep as the very nature of the mind." [4]
The Ultimate Cause of all is the omnipotent,
omnipresent Power that is active everywhere;
the eternal, unchangeable, all-pervasive substance in whom we live and move and have our
being; the God who is Love. This is more certain
than any other certainty. What the profoundest
theology of the age is asserting, that Evolution
corroborates and proves; that, in the language
of Dr. Newman Smyth, "Our rational consciousness is the inevitable resultant of the
powers, natural and spiritual, among which we
live, and which are always acting upon us.
We are ourselves personally present in the
omnipresence of God. We have our being in
Him, and our higher religious consciousness is
God's potential presence in the life of men." [5]
I doubt whether this "dynamical theism"
would ever have been arrived at if it had not
been for the influence of Evolution even upon

---

[4] First Principles. Cf. also Mr. Spencer's latest words on
the subject:

"One truth must ever grow clearer—the truth that there
is an Inscrutable Existence everywhere manifested, to which
he [man] can neither find nor conceive either beginning or
end. Amid the mysteries which become the more mysterious the more they are thought about, there will remain
the one absolute certainty, that he is ever in presence of an
Infinite and Eternal Energy, from which all things pro-
ceed."—*Ecclesiastical Institutions.*

[5] Andover Review, vol. i.

the theological world; and whether without this, men like Canon Fremantle would as readily have come to speak out the grand truth of a "God with us, God in us, God making himself a home in all the relations by which love and justice draw man to man, and class to class, and nation to nation; a God who is known and realized in the tenderness of fatherly and motherly and filial affection, the rapture of married love, the steadiness of friendship, the honesty of trade relations, the loyalty of citizenship, the righteousness of political rule, the peace which is destined to bind together all mankind. Where these exist there is God; where they are not He is absent." [6]

By the absolute certainty with which Evolution invests a few such fundamental facts as these of an almighty, beneficent Being, eternal, unchangeable, and immanent in the universe, and the vividness with which it shows him to our consciousness as a living actuality, it has done more for real, practical religion than could by any other means have been accomplished. What we lose in diffuseness we gain in depth of belief. In place of the many things offered our faith, we are given a few fundamental things upon which to concentrate our soul's powers. Instead of a multitude of more or less incongruous dogmas, in trying to adapt our inner

---

[6] The Gospel of the Secular Life.

and outer relations to which too much of our time and energy would have to be expended, and much of it in vain, we have a few simple facts as the alone essential ones with which our life has to be brought into harmony.

And we are enabled to do this the more readily by the further knowledge we are given of the mode of divine manifestation, and the manner and kind of the relations God sustains to the world. The sublime order by which "the heavens declare the glory of God," in which "day unto day uttereth speech, and night unto night showeth knowledge;" the order of the creation, the development, the government, the salvation of the universe; the method that is in the flight of the stellar flocks through space, in the vibration of the ether wavelets, the circulation of the sap of trees and blood of men; the laws ruling the spiritual sphere and reigning in the moral realm; all these are shown to be but the divine Presence existing and operating according to the constitution of his eternal being. In God's government there is no room for contingencies, there is no whim, no chance, no variableness nor shadow of turning. What the Scriptures ever sought to impress upon man, that Evolution succeeds in making him vividly realize. God reigns, not a man. All things consist according to beneficently inexorable law. Every cause has its effect; and no effect is without cause. Fire burns, always, everywhere, every one. Parallel lines never meet, on earth nor in heaven. "The wages of sin is death," ever, to all. Repent, and you are forgiven. "Believe and thou shalt be saved." We know God only by virtue of law. We can come to him only according to law. Ignoring law is ignoring God himself. Transgressing law is opposing God, is destroying self.

Of what great importance this knowledge is to practical religion will at once appear. It puts our striving after union with God on a new basis, and gives it a definite, intelligible direction. It does not change indeed any of the principles and rules of life given in the Bible; but it helps to explain them, and make us understand why they must be obeyed.

Before showing this more fully, however, one or two points of the clearer knowledge of human nature which Evolution emphasizes must be referred to. For they are as important as the knowledge of the divine, and must be taken in connection with it. Upon the two together depends the view we take of religion, of what it really consists, and how its end is to be reached.

The first of these points is the unity of human nature. The physical and the spritual parts of man cannot be separated and treated as wholly distinct. They are mutually dependent. Neither of them alone is man's self.

His reason, feeling, conscience, will, are affected largely by his digestion, the kind and quantity of his food, his home comforts, his par-
entage, his companionship, the climate, and his
environment in general. At the same time also
the former react upon the latter. The action,
reaction, and interaction of all these make up
his character, his self, the man. This fact has
been almost entirely ignored in theology. And
consequently also the further truth, or phase
of the same fact, that man is not only an individual unit, independent of all others, but is
a member of an organic whole. He is one of
many social units that together make up the
social organism. This on the one hand aids,
and on the other limits, his individual development. It cannot remain much below the aver-
age of the whole, nor can it rise far above it.
This greatly enlarges the aim and scope of
religion, and healthfully regulates its operations; making its true end not only the destruction of sins, but of sin; not only the redemption of men, but the salvation of man; not only
the bringing of persons into union with God,
but the bringing of all human relations and
institutions, of all humanity, into correspondence with divinity.

I do not mean to say that any of these facts
have been discovered by Evolution. They
have often been pointed out by philosophers
and theologians. But Evolution has brought

9

them into the unity of a system, and shown them to be the necessary outcome of fundamental principles deep down in the very nature of universal being. It has brought them into co-ordination with all other facts. And if those who at the present day are again laying stress upon them were not led to do it by the conscious or unconscious influence of Evolution, which is so mightily modifying all human thought, they at least will gain additional power to convince, if not greater certitude in their own minds, by finding them involved in the very principles of the dominant system and tendency of thought of the present time.

Bearing these truths with reference to the divine and the human natures in mind, we are now prepared, I think, to see in what that union or correspondence between God and man, which is true religion, consists, and how our striving for it can alone succeed.

Realizing the sublime truth of the immanence of God not only puts our consciousness of God upon the most solid and incontrovertible basis of absolute certainty, but it frees our conception of religion from that wholly artificial limitation that has grown up around it, and has done as much to hinder the religious progress of the world as all the opposition from without it has ever had to encounter. It is the pernicious notion that would cramp and confine all religion within the narrow bounds of ecclesiastical organization. Not that our principles do not allow the usefulness and importance of a thorough organization among believers. They grant this most freely. Human nature requires it. It is so greatly dependent upon its environment that it could not exist as religious without the strength that close fellowship with others gives, the help it derives from dogmas and disciplinary regulations, the inspiration and assistance obtained from forms of worship, seasons for instruction, meditation, prayer and praise, and the various hallowed associations afforded by the visible Church. But when, to use Mr. Spencer's words, "maintenance of the dogmas and forms of the religion becomes the primary, all-essential thing, and the secondary thing, often sacrificed, is the securing of those relations among men which the spirit of religion requires," ' then we protest against it. We protest against exalting this one means of religion into the chief if not the sole end; against the servant presuming to be the master; against ecclesiasticism taking the place of religion itself.

It is this abuse that has driven out of the Church hundreds of the greatest and best men the world has ever seen; just because they are so great. Their faith is too large to express itself in her symbols. Their character too many-sided to be adequately nourished at her

---

' The Study of Sociology.

meagre table. Their love too deep and glowing to find sufficient expression in her few forms
and ritual. Their religion is too full and complete. Thank God, however, she is not able to
drive such out of the true Church of Christ,
where men are received for what they *are*, not
only for what they think, or feel, or say, or
have. Where "He that doeth righteousness is
righteous." But none the less is it a great
harm to real, vital religion to be thus divided
asunder by an arbitrary line. There is no
authority in the language or spirit of the Scriptures for any such schism in the body of Christ,
any separation into sacred and secular such as
men have arrogantly made.

I am convinced that this whole abuse comes
from, or at least is maintained by, the narrow
and false view of God that obtains in the popular mind, however little it be sanctioned in the
formal theology of the present. He is not recognized as a Spirit suffused over all and through
the world. But he is localized somewhere; so
that one place is nearer to him than another.
And the Church is the nearest. He is fancied
to take more interest in some actions and relations than in others. And the relations of
church-membership, and exercises of church
worship, are the dearest to him. He must be
approached on the knees, addressed in hymns
and prayers, honored by special ceremonies.
Hence to join the Church is to "get religion;"

and to attend public worship is "divine service."
All else belongs to "secular life." Thus religion is made a distinct department of life in
contrast with all other departments like science,
or politics, art, education, or philosophy; and
too commonly in opposition and antagonism to
these. Well has Canon Fremantle in the volume before cited, expressed the sentiments that
alone accord with the principles of Evolution,
and are being more and more deeply felt by
thoughtful Christians: "The supposed antagonism between religion and the secular life is
not one which those who believe in God ought
to recognize. It is a form of dualism, with this
difference—that the old dualism was of good
and evil, this of two forms of good. But goodness is all one, and it is all divine and Christian.
Why should we separate from each other the
various manifestations of the same spirit? No
believer in God can really doubt that every
pure and unselfish development of human energy is consonant with the will and purpose of
God; nor that humanity and the world are
component parts of one great Unity; nor that
the elevation of humanity to its noblest and best
estate must be the aim of every man who lives
in earnest. And if there are those," he continues, "who think that religion is the enemy
of science or art or the political life, or of the
free exercise of criticism, or of political equality,
or of progress, we must endeavor to undeceive

them, just as we must undeceive religious men
who imagine that any of these tendencies are
in themselves anti-religious.''

Holding to the truth of the immanence of
God, we cannot degrade religion into merely
one of many rival occupations or departments
of life.   There is no such dualism as sacred and
secular.   All things are sacred in which the
divine manifests itself and operates.   Religion
is the tendency to bring all things into conformity and perfect harmony with the all-pres-
ent Spirit of God.   It exists in all literature that
aims to acquaint itself with and to express ''the
best which has been thought and said in the
world.''   It moves art to study and depict all
that is most beautiful, that it

> '' might touch the hearts of men,
> And bring them back to heaven again.''

It strives in politics to put the crown on righteousness, and give to justice the scepter where-
with to govern men.   With commerce it sails
o'er the seas to strengthen the brotherhood of
the race.——To science it gives the right to say,

> "My Father's works
> 'Tis mine to render plain to human thought.
> I war with Darkness, and I fight with Lies,
> I free the slave that Ignorance enthralls;
> I ferret hoar Delusion from his cave;
> I lift the veil from Superstition's eyes;
> I point the way to Truth wherever hid." [8]

---

[8] Venable—A Vision of Science.

With God everywhere near in real, living presence, religion is everywhere the reaching forth to touch him, to bring all departments of life into the divine mould, all human operations into harmony with the divine activity. How can there be any opposition between them? Or what right has one to say, I have religion; ye have not? "For the body is not one member, but many. . . . . And the eye cannot say unto the hand, I have no need of thee: nor again, the head to the feet, I have no need of you. Nay, much more, those members of the body, which seem to be more feeble, are necessary."

The great need of the world to-day is to realize the universal immanence of God as Ruler, Guide, Saviour; of him who declared, "Lo, I am with you alway, even to the end of the world;" not to heed the cry Lo, here! or Lo, there, is Christ! but to accept the fact that the kingdom of heaven is within the heart. When I see how much of the means of the Church is expended on the mere maintenance of ecclesiastical government, its ministry and machinery, the building and ornamentation of its houses of worship; how inordinately large a proportion of its time and energy is given to such purely subjective exercises as are demanded by its public services, its preaching, supplications, and adoration, to say nothing of its conferences, synods, and controversies, compared with its activity in more practical, objective directions; I cannot but confess that there is almost more religion in the so-called secular world than in the Church. Look at the God-ward tendency, the religious agencies, that are manifesting themselves in the application of science to the bodily, intellectual, and moral elevation of mankind; the improvement of men's health, their food, their clothing, their dwellings, the facilities of intercourse between them, the cure of their ailments, the increase of their usefulness and happiness, and the removal of those physical hinderances at least that stand in the way of their attaining to a perfect manhood, to eternal life! Look at the homes and hospitals and asylums "the world" is building; at the interest politics are manifesting in the cause of temperance, chastity, official purity, education, and civilization! Notice the innumerable "secular" organizations for humanitarian purposes; the work literature is doing, and art, for the highest spiritual enlightenment, and ethical as well as æsthetical culture of man! True religion is mightily stirring and strenuously laboring in all these various directions; and certainly if the Church do not soon wake up to an adequate sense of her great privilege, facilities, and duty, she will be left in the rear instead of being the leader of the universal God-ward movement.

I am jealous for the Church. I believe that she can and ought to be at the very head of all religious agencies. Therefore I am anxious that she should speedily enlarge her borders, pull down the walls of partition that now so wrongfully separate her from the multitude of other religious forces that are everywhere working so mightily, and embrace and heartily join hands with righteousness, goodness, and truth wherever found. She was never meant to be confined to the few partial phases of religious activity she now displays; never designed to be a mere conserver of dogma and forms of worship ''abstracted from the common life of men.'' ''Its power is not that of a distant God who must be approached by special ceremonies, by special modes of life and thought, by shaping humanity into some peculiar attitude, but the power of a present God. The title of its Founder is Immanuel. '

If this is once fully realized, I believe that the ''Church of the Future,'' so eloquently pictured by Dr. Washington Gladden, in one of his sermons, will become an actual fact. ''Large and wise enterprises for the welfare of men will be set on foot, many of the instrumentalities now in use will continue to be employed, under modified forms, and many new ones will be devised. It will be understood that the law of the Church is simply this, 'Let us do good to all men as we have opportunity.'

' Fremantle—Gospel of the Secular Life.

No means of making men better will be counted
unlawful; everything that helps to lift them
out of misery and bring them near to God will
be received with thanksgiving. . . . . In
short, the Church of the Future, loyal to its
great Head, and leaning on his counsel and his
might, will go out into the world and take
possession of it, in his name. Wherever there
are wrongs it will strive to right them; wherever there are needs it will work to supply them;
wherever there are sorrows it will love to comfort them; wherever there are any whom Christ
would have helped, it will go to them and
carry the gifts he came to bring." Read also
what Dr. Phillips Brooks has recently spoken,
when in addressing the Harvard Divinity School
he said, "The great mass of men do not to-day
belong in associated relations with the Christian
Church. What does that mean? First, that
the Christian Church has not made itself broad
enough to make earnest and true men recognize
the ideal of their humanity in it; that it has
been too special, too fantastic. Secondly, that
it has a great work before it so to declare its
human application that it shall commend itself
to every man who really is in earnest in his
thought, and earnest in his deed. The Church
seems to me to have that great function before
it, and never to have had the possibility for the
fulfillment of that duty so large and open before
it, in all the ages of its existence as to-day."

The very fact that there are men within it who can speak such words, and do speak them, is to me a most significant and helpful sign.

While the Church that would have the sympathy and co-operation of those who are influenced by the principles and modes of thought of Evolution must do all this, while she dare not refuse to do it if she would keep up with the truer interpretation of Scripture that is ever being more widely accepted, she will not by any means have to pay less attention to what are called the "means of grace." She will, however, if these are to serve their proper purpose, be obliged to rid the minds of the people more thoroughly of many of the heathen notions with which they regard and use them. This will be possible if the real all-presence of God is once fully appreciated. Then his immutability will be properly understood; and it will be seen that his spiritual laws as his physical laws, are not mere commands or decrees imposed by him for the regulation of the world, but simply the infinitely varied modes of his being. To change the slightest detail of any one of them would be nothing less than to change the whole constitution and being of God himself. This is unthinkable, utterly and absolutely impossible; and nowhere more positively declared such than in the Bible, though it was left to Evolution to explain the fact, to demonstrate and anew insist upon it.

Now it will not be denied, by any one acquainted with popular religious thought, that in nearly all current worship this impossibility is entirely ignored, and its opposite taken for granted. The heathen idea that worship is intended to change the attitude of God toward the worshipper is still all too prevalent. The necessity of correspondence between the human and the divine is indeed felt; but it is sought to be effected by bringing God into conformity with man! The bulk of the devotees in our churches, taking literally such expressions as "pleasing, propitiating, glorifying God," actually imagine that their songs of praise—especially if artistically rendered by a professional choir!—cause pleasurable sensations in the consciousness of the Deity, in return for which they will be made the recipients of special favors from him. They fancy that their eloquent petitions,—whether intoned by a deep sonorous voice that brings out the rhythmical beauty of a symmetrical litany, or shouted in hoarse tones from the stentorian throat of a class-leader,— will touch the feelings of God, and move him to do what otherwise he would not have done, —which in one sense is not without truth, but not in their sense. They believe that their presence in the church edifice,—whether it be a Gothic pile of white marble, or a cabin of rough-hewn logs,—will change God's sentiments, thoughts, and conduct towards them.

With this in view they engage in these devo-
tions. They are thoroughly sincere, the most
of them. They really love their idea of God,
therefore they wish to please him and to contribute to his glory. They feel their dependence upon him deeply, hence their efforts to
propitiate and conciliate him. But they know
him so imperfectly that they only succeed in
degrading him, and in causing offence and dis-
gust to those more spiritually minded.

The comparative emptiness of our churches is
not a sign of indifference to religion; but a
protest of the reverent intelligence of men
against its abuse and misapplication. It is the
modern echo of Samuel's rebuke, "Behold, to
obey is better than sacrifice;" the reiteration
of Isaiah's inspiration, "Bring no more vain
oblations: incense is an abomination unto me;
the new moons and sabbaths, the calling of
assemblies, I cannot away with. . . . . .
Wash you, make you clean; cease to do evil;
learn to do well; seek judgment, relieve the
oppressed; judge the fatherless; plead for the
widow;" the repetition of Paul's sentiments on
Mars' Hill, "The God who made the world
and all things therein, he that is Master of
heaven and of earth not in hand-made temples
dwells, neither by hands of men is served, as
though he needed anything; he that gives to
all life, and breath, and all things." As such
it is indeed being recognized by the most truly

religious and spiritual men of our times, by men like Dr. Lyman Abbott, for instance, who declares that "Agnosticism is a protest against idolatry; and a true protest;" and who thus paraphrases Paul's words to apply to our own times: "Away with your conceptions and ideas of God, which are but subtle idols; away with your notion that your service counts for aught; as though he needed anything. Away with your narrow and narrowing thought that he dwells in hand-made temples, and that those only seek him who go to church and accept the preacher's pictures as a photographic likeness." [10]

True worship must have just the opposite basis from that described, and then will both fulfill its proper purpose, and not repel so many of the best men as it does now. It is simply one of many means to further religion, to help man to conform himself to God. As such it is necessary, and demanded as indispensable on the principles of Evolution itself. It is a medium of expression and means of strengthening the religious sentiments. It is a bond of spiritual union, helping to draw believers more closely together. It supplies motive-power, instruction, and guidance to enable men the better to fulfill the end of religion. In no other way now known, or practicable, than by the ser-

---

[10] The Christian Union.

mon, the exposition and application of the
Scriptures, would men come as thoroughly to
understand and as often to be reminded of
those eternal principles upon which their lives
must be built, and be instructed in the rules for
the practical guidance of life, how they must
live, what they must do, to come into union
with God; and in no other would they be as
strongly moved to do it, would their motives
be so enkindled, and their desire and longing
for union with the divine be so freshened,
strengthened, and perpetuated. No, the sermon,—the sermon as it should be perhaps rather
than the sermon as it is,—can never be abol-
ished, however its name and form may be
changed.

And just as little the united praise and prayer
which cluster around it. The divine power
that swells through the strains of truly devo-
tional music is not only a grand means of giving
expression to sentiments of trust and hope and
adoration; but it reacts in filling the heart with
firmer trust, with larger hope, with more ar-
dent praise. It purifies and elevates the soul.
It generates new motives and working power.
The united exercise of prayer is an inspiration
in itself. While expressing man's wants and
sorrows and holiest aspirations it supplies the
divine force for their satisfaction. It makes
definite the yearnings of the heart; submissive
and obedient the will; peaceful and strong the

whole being.   What the deep-sighted Hindoo
Mozoomdar said of the Praying Christ, is true
of every Christian who rightly prays.   "The
attitude of uplooking faith is the chief medium
through which the mind of God can be poured
into the devotee's mind.   By the vision of instinctive trust, the praying Jesus first beheld
what was in the purpose of the Father, and
then prayed for the fulfillment of that purpose."
Thus "The unity of will with will, deepened
by faith, love, and obedience, made his prayers
natural and incessant.   Such prayer made his
activity instantaneous, and that activity was
crowned with the miracles of success." [11]
Surely such devotion is never to be surrendered.

As far as these and all other forms of worship are engaged in with a clear perception of
their true relation and efficacy to religion, they
are useful and even essential.   They with the
whole system of ecclesiasticism belong to the
environment upon which man depends, in his
present stage of development, as a religious
being;—upon which he depends to bring himself into full correspondence and harmony with
that Being who is perfect Love, an ever-present
Love, manifesting himself in the beneficence of
that wondrous order which we call law; which,
if we could change, could only become less
perfectly beneficent; which, if we would fully

---

[11] The Oriental Christ.

enjoy, we need only bring ourselves into full conformity with. It is not conditioned for its existence or operation by aught that we can do. But we are for our enjoyment of it, for our whole spiritual life, dependent upon the degree of our inner and outer adjustment to it. "Herein is love, not that we loved God, but that he loved us;" and "we love him because first he loved us."

If religion, further, is the bringing of man into correspondence with the divine, of the whole man, all the principles of his being and activities of his life, then surely can it not be regarded, as it is by many, as a mere acceptance of a system of doctrines; nor yet, as by others, as nothing more than a matter of the sentiments and emotions. As the true conception of God removes the objective limitations ecclesiasticism would impose, so does the view Evolution gives of man's being and nature deny these subjective limitations. Religion cannot be relegated to any one faculty or set of faculties, nor for that matter to any other part only of man. Man is indeed essentially one; but he has many sides, physical, intellectual, emotional, moral. Unless all these sides are fitted to the divine order of being, his religion will be but partial and imperfect. Only the co-ordination of all these with the divine and with one another, can make the man's self religious. This depends equally upon all.

Yet there are those who would make it depend wholly upon the intellectual faculties alone. He who can most positively subscribe to his creed, is most skillful in defending it by argument and Scripture quotations, and most zealous in guarding it against innovation and "new ideas," he is the most religious man. Righteousness with them is to believe the right doctrine; sin, to be unable or unwilling to believe what this or that authority has declared to be the correct thing. So that I know men the most rigidly orthodox who are at the same time the most uncharitable, unforgiving, unhopeful, un-Christlike and unreligious within my acquaintance. Well does Dr. Smyth protest against such mere dogmatists, in the paper from which I have already quoted, that "Christianity is not primarily a system of doctrines arranged in rational order, but a system of beings in right relation to God and in harmony with each other." Indeed so strong is the reaction against mere intellectualism in religion showing itself, especially in the so-called "New Theology," that I am in hopes it will soon have passed away entirely.

Perhaps there is danger that this very reaction may strengthen the equally partial and crippling view, that obtains so largely in the popular conception and practice, and which would make the feelings the sole legitimate and only needed sphere of religion. Made current in theology chiefly through the perversion of Schleiermacher's teachings, it was perhaps but the natural revulsion against the cold and barren rationalism that too long had tyrannized the Christian world. It was given strength by the Scottish school of philosophy, which through Brown, Hamilton, Mansel, and their class, insisted on a special faith-faculty, spoke only of religious sentiments, and practically revived the nonsense of Tertullian's famous "*Certum est quia impossibile est.*" From this school Herbert Spencer and many of his followers adopted the notion, along with the "Law of the Unconditioned." So that Evolution has come to be blamed for holding that the reason can have no part in religion whatever which is the province of the sensibilities alone.

Whether this was its foundation or not, certain it is that in our popular religion the feelings are well-nigh the only part of the mind that is brought into play. Go into almost any church of a Sunday and you will at once see how true this is. Everything there, from the architecture to the dress of the clergy, including the sermon itself, appeals to your sympathy, your ambition, your fear, sorrow, joy, admiration, affection; but to how little else! What is there provided for the reason, the thinking powers, the conscience, for the guidance of the life and formation of the whole character? It is simply a fact that of a very

large part of the current Christianity of to-day
it may be said as truly as it has been of the
religion of the old Puranas, that "Never
was there a more complete example of piety
divorced from morality than in these theories."
Abundant and sad experience with these emotional religionists would alone be enough to
make us heartily agree with Dr. George Harris,
when he said in his notable Inaugural Address
at Andover, that "It is of the last importance
that we do not relinquish or think slightingly
of the office of reason in the recognition of religious truth.   To maintain that doctrine is received by feeling or by a faith-faculty, and
not primarily by reason, is to surrender to the
enemy without discretion. . . . .   In order
to assert the right use of feeling and faith we
are not required to discredit reason.   Indeed
faith is the highest exercise of reason, and feeling glows by gazing on the object which reason
apprehends."

The truth is that reason and the feelings are
alike concerned, as being two sides of human
nature, equally important in the moulding of
the man and in the expression of his self.   They
are two of the main avenues through which the
divine Love impresses itself on us when radiated
through Christ, helping to generate the new
principle of life within us, to start a new process
of adjustments and adaptations of inner and
outer relations, and thus to effect the formation

of a new character, a new creature, responsive to every manifestation of God within and without, obedient to every breath of the Spirit, every throb of the divine Being, living in unison with God's life, freed from the forces of sin and of death, secure in the Eternal Life.

But neither of the two alone, nor both the reason and the feelings together, are the only root-channels of this divine communion, as they are not the only roots of the character-trunk; they are only the conscious ones. But the unconscious are more numerous, and, in their aggregate at least, equally strong and important. This is the truth, of vast practical import, that the world must yet learn and use to a far fuller extent than it has thus far done, if the kingdoms of this world are ever to become the kingdoms of our Lord and of his Christ.

Its neglect is the fruitful source of much of the deplorable inconsistency among believers, which gives their foes so great offence and frequent occasion for just reproach. It explains why "there is none righteous, no, not one." For while this one may have one, two, or half a dozen of the roots of his being connected with God, this connection may be lacking entirely, or be very imperfect, with respect to the others. He may be thoroughly orthodox, but wholly unloving. Or his emotional nature may be very fully conformed with the divine goodness, while intellectually he is decidedly heterodox. Or both intellectually and sentimentally he may be out of the divine harmony, but by inheritance and training have been brought into unconscious correspondence with God so far as the practical side of his character is concerned; he will be by nature a "moral man." None of these will be consistent Christians,—as who of us is? Each one of them will be only partially religious. But has any one of them a right to say to the others, You are not Christians? Dare the orthodox charge the emotional one with impiety? Or either accuse him who is merely "good by nature" with ungodliness? Who shall presume to say which of them is most perfectly religious, seeing that the religion of each is defective? Let none venture it, lest he hear the merited rebuke of the alone Perfect One, "Thou hypocrite, first cast out the beam out of thine own eye; and then shalt thou see clearly to cast out the mote out of thy brother's eye."

Nor is this only a rebuke. It indicates also the true method of religious culture in so far. The too prevalent method is to labor with zeal in discovering and correcting the defects of others, and in trying to convince them of our excellences and to secure their adoption. Once in a while we succeed, and then straightway imagine we are converting the world! The "more excellent way" is for us to search out the good that is in others, cheerfully to acknowledge and gladly to adopt it, complementing therewith our own. Such we are shown, in the article before quoted, by Dr. Lyman Abbott, than whom none is more competent to speak on the subject, was the method of the greatest of the Apostles, and such would be his way were he living to-day. "He would not ransack the writings of Huxley, and Tyndall, and Spencer to prove them atheists. He would ransack them for a different purpose. He would try not to make the worst, but the best out of them. He who quoted, not Lucretius but Aratus and Cleanthes, would find evidences of theism, not of atheism, in modern philosophy and modern science. He would not refuse to welcome Mozoomdar because he was not an orthodox Trinitarian; he would look in Matthew Arnold not for sentences against inspiration, but for sentences witnessing to a living God; he would cite the last page of Huxley's monograph on Hume as a testimony—in some sense, an unconscious testimony—to the trustworthiness of spiritual perception; he would find in Herbert Spencer's favorite phrase, the Unknown and the Unknowable, unintentional witness of consciousness to the Infinite One, in whom we all live and move and have our being, and whom, therefore, we all recognize in spite of ourselves. He would cull even from Robert Ingersoll, not his worst blasphemies, but his reluctant testimonies to the Divine in man and about man." This the wisest method of charity would not only enrich ourselves, but would do more than by any other can be done to perfect the religion of others.

It would bring to bear upon them the powerful force of example. Because we would show ourselves first willing frankly to examine their excellences, they would be willing to do the same to ours. This alone would be great gain. If we could only get the thoughtful attention of honest and pure characters, we could. leave the rest to the convincing power of the truth itself.

> " Truth needs no champions: in the infinite deep
> Of everlasting Soul her strength abides."

If there is truth in our religion, the true soul will see it, be drawn to it, absorb it. The chief difficulty is to get men's attention, to get them earnestly to examine it. But I believe this difficulty would vanish if we ourselves would first set the example of ingenuousness towards them. Certainly much sooner than by our constantly looking upon them with suspicion and even supercilious pride. It is neglect of the Saviour's injunction that has hindered the progress of the world as much as anything else. Not the stubbornness of the world any more than the stubbornness of Christians has set the two classes against each other, and filled the earth with sounds of crimination and recrimination, condemnation and defiance, instead of enthroning

the Prince of Peace over all, and bringing
everywhere peace on earth and good will towards men.

Immense as would be the gain if by the
method of charity all good men and true would
thus join hearts and hands, and become laborers
together with God, it would be but an inci-
dental blessing accruing from the recognition of
the truth of the many-sided unity of man, which
Evolution has anew emphasized, and of its significance to religion. Let Christians grasp it
firmly and the whole armory of the universe is
thrown open to them, with all its infinite variety of weapons and implements. Whatever
goes to the forming of a man is given into their
hands, so to use as to form him in the image of
God. How few and puny now appear the
agencies which are employed in this glorious
work! No wonder the progress has been so
slow, and the results so meager and unsatisfac-
tory! We have tried preaching our sermons
and saying our prayers in a hundred thousand
churches in our land; but it has not kept a
million dram-shops and gambling hells and
bawdy houses from building against their very
walls. We have spent four million dollars in
erecting sumptuous houses of worship; but they
do not bring shelter and food to the thousands
of freezing and starving ones at their doors. We
have sought to win heathendom for Christ
through the reason and the feelings alone, and

have succeeded in gaining the ears of scarcely
two millions of pagans, while more than ten
hundred millions have not been reached. In
ten years we have expended perhaps one hundred millions of money in sending preachers and
teachers, tracts and hymn-books and Bibles into
our Home Mission field to win the land for
righteousness; but to-day intemperance every
year sends nine hundred million dollars on its
mission of death, and gleefully points to the
hundred thousand graves it annually digs for
its victims. In spite of all we have done, Mor-
monism is still as united and defiant as ever
before; its ally, the "social evil" in our midst,
leers upon us more boldly; political corruption
is more strongly entrenched; unclean literature
grows more insinuating, more artistic and
dangerous; and pauperism keeps on breeding
crime and misery to a more alarming extent
than ever in the past.

The very magnitude of these evils, the very
intricacy of these complex social problems, that
press so menacingly upon us for solution, is
forcing the truth upon us that, if Christianity
is ever successfully to meet them, it must be in
other ways, by more and mightier agencies,
besides the few limited ones it thus far has employed. It must take to heart more fully the
teaching of Paul, that in this work "there are
diversities of gifts . . . and there are differences of administrations . . . and there

are diversities of operations; but it is the same God which worketh all in all."

Who ever heard of a fortress being taken by a mere succession of cavalry charges,—and that by platoons? It is what Christianity is trying to do. It charges straight against the citadels of evil, armed only with the sword of the spirit; charges in open daylight, in full uniform, after duly notifying the enemy that it is coming! The results show that we have tried these unwise tactics long enough. Our work has been altogether one-sided and only superficial. Forgetful of the admonition that "that was not first which is spiritual, but that which is natural; and afterwards that which is spiritual," we have commenced with and confined ourselves to the latter alone; have struggled with results instead of with causes; have worked at the surface, and not at the center; tried to dip up the foul stream of sin at its mouth, instead of going to its source.

A recent writer in the *Christian Union* has words on this point which are as wise as they are significant of the needs of the hour. The world is coming to demand that Christianity should rise up to its capabilities, and laying the axe at the root of the tree, should do its whole duty. "I see no hope," he says, "of a regenerated future on this planet except Christianity can push its principles and life back through ethical and legal channels so as to purify the physical sources of life. This I believe it is amply competent to do when it shall bend its energies mainly to saving the 'life that now is,' and to saving it in its entirety, as a physical, moral, and spiritual entity, here and beyond; for if this world is well taken care of, the next will take care of itself." Experience is adding its voice to call for what the teachings of Script-ure and of Evolution alike insist upon. In the divine work of lifting man up to God, whether as an individual or as a social organism, we must use all means; every conscious and uncon-scious influence, every spiritual and physical agency, furnished by God, must be employed in the service of religion.

For the individual, for instance, besides the means we now almost exclusively use, we must enlist also the myriad agencies that are alive and active in every one's environment. With them we can mightily facilitate the new birth. It is vain to ask God to create a clean heart in a body that is habitually encrusted with filth. Make outward cleanliness to surround it first, and the pure heart will be possible which only can see God. While the hunger and thirst for bread and meat are pinching and exhausting the physical frame, there is no room in con-sciousness for that hunger and thirst after righteousness which the Spirit satisfies. Shiv-ering in scanty rags, the robe of Jesus' right-eousness will be refused for a more material

garment to warm the flesh and bones. In a
dingy, dark hovel, adorned by nothing but loud
prints of half-nude actresses on the walls,
"Police Gazettes" on the table, and ribald songs
in the air, there is small likelihood of the beauty
of holiness being appreciated. We must dis-
tribute soap, food, clothing, coal, as well as
tracts and Bibles. We must pay more heed to
the physical conditions, the material soil out of
which the fruits of the spirit are to grow. If
the soil be not first prepared, nearly all the seed
we sow thereon will be utterly wasted.

And just so with the growth in grace. The
new-born man must be fed and nourished
through every channel, with food adapted to
every organ and part of the "physical, moral,
and spiritual entity," so that the whole charac-
er may be truly converted to God and developed
in God into a symmetrical, well-rounded man.
All the time we must remember that while
every individual is a unity, he is also an organic
member of the social body. "And whether
one member suffer, all the members suffer with
it; or one member be honored, all the members
rejoice with it." We may therefore not look
for completeness, perfection of religiousness in
the individual; but must expect all the others
to eke out, to complement, the imperfections
and defects of each. Social environment must
be made the efficient factor it is meant to be,
strengthening righteous incentives, furnishing

needed restraints, cheering, helping all. And in return this organism is itself made by so much more religious as each new religious member is an added point in it of the union with God.

Not only for the individual's sake, therefore, but also for the world's, our energies need to be bent more earnestly and intelligently than has thus far been done directly to the regeneration of the whole social and race organism. The recognition of this truth more fully than was done before, by the most advanced theologians and Christian workers of the present, is one of the most hopeful signs of a more enlightened religious life for the future. And I am convinced it is one of the good fruits already visible of the application of the principles of Evolution to the work of Christianity,—if unconscious not therefore less real. The "New Theology," for instance, according to Dr. Munger, "turns our attention to the corporate life of man in the world,—an individual life, indeed, but springing from common roots, fed by a common life, watched over by one Father, inspired by one Spirit, and growing to one end; no man, no generation, being 'made perfect' by itself. Hence its ethical emphasis; hence its recognition of the nation, and of the family, and of social and commercial life, as fields of the manifestation of God and of the operation of the Spirit; hence its readiness to ally itself with all movements for bettering the condition of mankind,

—holding that human society itself is to be redeemed, and that the world itself, in its corporate capacity, is being reconciled with God." [12]

Fully realizing this, Christians will aim at larger results than the mere regeneration of individual, matured sinners; and therefore will use larger and more radical means, besides those it now employs. Not content with snatching here and there a brand from the burning, they will take measures also for quenching the fire itself. For instance, they will engage the services of that vast array of subtle forces involved in the principle of heredity. Now they are allowed to obey almost without hinderance the degenerative law of reversion that makes for sin and death. Where we succeed in converting one sinner, these supply his place by a dozen new ones, in whom the poison-germs of vice and crime are inborn, spawned in the million reeking dens and hovels of our cities, producing new generations of beings more degraded and vicious than the old. The conditions under which their production is made so terribly great must be destroyed. Religious teaching alone will not do it. It must be complemented by religious laws, religious architecture, religious feeding, by every means that will tend to purify the fountains of human life and society that now are almost hopelessly befouled.

---

[12] The Freedom of Faith—Introd.

Whatever human institutions help to foster and sustain ignorance and poverty, with their commonly attendant evils of intemperance, filth, unchastity, indolence, physical and moral unhealthiness, by so much help to beget and bear a class of society whose rapid growth is one of the greatest dangers of our country, and one of the most fatal obstacles to its religious advancement. And whatever agencies and measures, therefore, will tend to remove such ignorance and poverty, and to remove the conditions of domestic infidelity and unhappiness, intemperance and evil,—and there are many others besides poverty and ignorance—such agencies are to be freely, strongly employed in the name of religion and of Christ. Their past neglect has been the weakness and the reproach of Christianity. The divine Love and Righteousness must be allowed to work through the political, educational, medical, mercantile, and all other institutions that mould and shape society, the nation, and the race. The Spirit of God must control these as directly and fully as he must control all else. The more he does this, the more will individuals be brought under his saving sway. It is a truth just as certain as the other, that the more individuals are religious, the more religious will the whole social body be. The two go together. One is as true and as important as the other. And what a field it gives for Christian effort and labor! What a

host of possible allies! What a store of new
and mighty weapons! Aye, and how large and
glorious a hope it sets before the earnest disciple!

Will the field ever be fully occupied? Will
the allies ever be enlisted; the new weapons
and forces applied; this glorious hope be ever
realized?

Certainly not so long as Christianity and
Evolution are made to appear as antagonistic
and contradictory systems. But when once
evolutionists shall be consistent enough frankly
to confess that their system without God, the
Father, the Son, and the Holy Spirit, without
the facts of Providence and prayer, of sin and
salvation, is incomplete and erroneous; and
shall be willing, consciously as they already do
unconsciously, to accept the principles of Christianity as the necessary complement of their
own, and its motive and end as the essential
realities that alone render intelligible and of
practical worth that sublime method which
their system so clearly sets forth; then will
they no longer refuse to embrace religion, nor
confound it with mere superstition unworthy of
rational men. They will see that Christians are
laboring with them in working out the eternal
destinies of the world; and will freely join
hands in the common task. And on the other
hand, when once Christians shall have faith
enough to acknowledge, with that one of their

humber who has most carefully examined the structural principles of Evolution, that it is "The Via Sacra of the universe; the road along which the Blessed One walked forth, first in Creative power and majesty, then in loving providential care, then in higher wisdom and goodness, foreshadowing what He was about to do, and finally along this path reached His Cross, and there consummated that sacrifice by which alone His infinite love was revealed;"[13] then will they no longer suspect and fear and hate the system as ungodly and sinful, but see in it only another form of expressing the essential truth they ever have held. Then will each strengthen the other; and both together go forth in a more earnest and effective warfare than ever yet has been waged against the united hordes of blind error and ignorance and hosts of evil and sin. Then will indeed victory soon perch on the banners of Truth, and the time not be so far distant as now, when the knowledge of God shall cover the earth as the waters cover the sea.

---

[13] W. D. Ground—Examination of Struct'l Principles of Spencer's Philosophy.

FINIS.

INDEX OF AUTHORS.

www.ingramcontent.com/pod-product-compliance
Lightning Source LLC
Chambersburg PA
CBHW020852020726
47497CB00005B/1364